Democratic Organization for Social Change

DEMOCRATIC ORGANIZATION FOR SOCIAL CHANGE

Latin American Christian Base Communities and Literacy Campaigns

JOHANNES P. VAN VUGT

BERGIN & GARVEY

New York • Westport, Connecticut • London

Copyright Acknowledgments

The author and the publisher are grateful to the following for granting use of their material:

R. Arnove, *Education and Revolution in Nicaragua* (New York: Praeger, 1986). Reprinted by permission of Praeger Publishers.

D. Barbe, *Grace and Power* (Maryknoll, NY: Orbis Books, 1987). Reprinted by permission of Orbis Books.

EDUCATION FOR CRITICAL CONSCIOUSNESS by Paulo Freire. Copyright © 1973 by Paulo Freire. Reprinted by permission of the Continuum Publishing Company.

J. Marins, *Comunidades eclesial de base: curso fundamental* (Buenos Aires: Editorial Bonum, 1972). Reprinted by permission of Editorial Bonum.

Library of Congress Cataloging-in-Publication Data

Van Vugt, J. P.
   Democratic organization for social change : Latin
American Christian base communities and literacy campaigns /
Johannes P. Van Vugt.
     p. cm.
   Includes bibliographical references and index.
   ISBN 0–89789–245–3
   1. Basic Christian communities—Latin America—Case studies.
2. Literacy programs—Latin America—Case studies. 3. Social
history—Latin America—Case studies. I. Title.
BX2347.72.L37V84   1991
307.77′4′09728—dc20   90–1132

British Library Cataloguing in Publication Data is available.

Copyright © 1991 by Johannes P. Van Vugt

Library of Congress Catalog Card Number: 90–1132
ISBN: 0–89789–245–3

First published in 1991

Bergin & Garvey, One Madison Avenue, New York, NY 10010
An imprint of Greenwood Publishing Group, Inc.

Printed in the United States of America

The paper used in this book complies with the
Permanent Paper Standard issued by the National
Information Standards Organization (Z39.48-1984).

10 9 8 7 6 5 4 3 2 1

This book is dedicated to all
who have given their lives for democracy and freedom.

Contents

Preface

On November 16, 1989, six Jesuit priests, their housekeeper and her daughter were dragged from their residence at a Catholic university in San Salvador and executed—undoubtedly by death squad members acting with the consent of the military and government of El Salvador (Rivera y Damas 1989). The priests, faculty and administrators of the University of Central America, had been accused of being leftist intellectuals, Communists, and collaborators with the guerrillas who have been fighting a civil war with the military and government of El Salvador for over a decade. The government is kept in power by vast sums of military aid, over one million dollars daily, from the government of the United States of America. This military aid was briefly suspended by the presidency of Jimmy Carter after the assassination of El Salvador's Archbishop Oscar Romero in 1980. With the election of Ronald Reagan military aid was resumed in full force, despite the murder of four church women by the government-related death squads. No senior officials have been properly brought to trial for the murders of these religious. The current archbishop of El Salvador has accused the Federal Bureau of Investigation (FBI) of brainwashing and intimidating the only witness of the assassinations at the university.

Much has been said in the media and in government and Church circles of the political impact of liberation theology and Christian or Church Base Communities (*Comunidades Eclesia de Base*, CEB) and literacy campaigns in Latin America. These statements have resulted in stereotypes in the minds of many Americans. The neoconservative and more radical right claims that the CEBs are more Communist than Christian, that they foment discontent and revolution, and that they are the works of the devil. Pope John Paul II has variously silenced liberation theologians and censured or curtailed the ecclesial authority of politically involved liberationist clergy. The United States has withdrawn support from the United Nations Educational, Scientific, and Cultural Organization (Unesco), which lauded revolutionary Nicaragua's literacy campaign. For their part, liberation theologians and those allied with the Church of the Poor defend the popular Church, the CEBs, as an attempt to revitalize the Church by following Christ's preferential option for the poor. They claim the traditional Church is corrupted by its complicity in the institutionalized violence which has left the majority in Latin America poor, and getting poorer. Likewise, educational theorists propose literacy campaigns that, instead of fostering cultural reproduction, would challenge the injustices of the status quo: using education as a means to name the causes of oppression experienced by a community. Liberation advocates argue that by organizing base communities and learning circles, communities would be able to learn, demand, and defend their rights against governments held in power by repression and U.S. military aid, governments which contribute to the further dispossession of their own populaces for the sake of increased profits for a ruling oligarchy, a few large landholders, and multinational corporations.

Liberationist pedagogues and theologians have written their theoretical tracts. Many books have been written on the theologies of liberation by missionary pastors involved in CEB formation. Political scientists have often written books on how these unfortunate populations, including their churches, are caught between two fires, the political interests of the United States and the Soviet Union, and that the churches, and their theologians, are merely pawns in this global chess match. Other social scientists, notably macrosociologists, argue that the churches and congregations are pawns of a larger economic system, the capitalist world system, and its effect on shifting local modes of production. Anthropologists have tried to articulate the belief systems of revolutionaries and how they interface with traditional belief systems. Few, however, have tried to treat the so called pawns—peasant farmers, displaced urban unemployed, and their pastors—as independent actors, freely and consciously choosing between the many forces at play in their lives.

For the sake of analysis and in response to the stereotypes, but at the risk of adding to the oversimplification of a complex reality, lines need to be clearly drawn: Are the CEBs instruments which empower their participants through an increased self-direction or are they tools of Communist, subversive, and revolutionary indoctrination? More political mudslinging does not seem to be the way to provide any further clarification of the issue. Rather, as a social scientist, I propose that by looking at the issue from the micro-level of the individual actors involved, reconstructing as far as possible their actions and motives, perhaps some clarification can be offered and the roots of the accusations identified.

To do so, in any kind of convincing scientific manner, involves measurement by an objective means, with all of the limitations that current debates in the philosophy of science place on that objectivity. It involves realizing one's own biases as well as the selective attention to one's instruments of measure, one's limitations, and those of one's science. For this reason my style may appear to be overly cautious, academic, and pedantic. It is in itself a formidable task, involving the necessity to acknowledge, if not adequately deal with, the macro- as well as the micro-forces involved in recognizing the complexity of social change. In the end I hope at least to have contributed to an understanding of the role of the CEBs and literacy campaigns in attempts at social change in Latin America.

Utilizing field research in Nicaragua and secondary research on El Salvador, Guatemala, and Brazil (much of the work using Latin American sources), and theories of democratic organization and social change, I seek to measure, in a scientific manner, whether the literacy campaigns of Nicaragua and Brazil, and the CEBs of the four countries, are democratic or a means of Communist indoctrination; and if so to what degree. Some claim they are sincere efforts at social transformation by empowering the marginalized and disenfranchised to participate in their self-direction. Others have made implicit and explicit accusations of these efforts. These accusations are used to justify the assassination of religious and to withhold funds from Unesco. It seems apparent to me, as a scientist, that the way to address these claims and accusations is to begin with a clear definition, setting up a model of what a democratic organization engaged in social transformation would look like, and then measuring the reality of the literacy campaigns and CEBs by this model.

This is what I do in my research. Further, by making it comparative, noting the circumstances under which such democratic organizations are compromised, fall short of the ideal or fail, and circumstances under which they succeed, it is possible to identify what circumstances are limiting, and have limited, these attempts at democratic organization for social transformation, whether it be the leaders' efforts at indoctrination or harassment by external authorities. By employing this model, scientific measure provides a guide through a complex and controversial subject while avoiding polemics and apologetics.

Presumptuously, I hope, by treating this subject as a case study, to contribute to scientific method and theory in answering a persistent problem in social change: How is a local-level democratic organization cultivated so that members, who were previously disenfranchised, are empowered to oppose an oppressive central authority and participate in a revolutionary reconstruction of society? This research seeks to answer this question by constructing a model of democratic organization for social transformation. This model is constructed by moving dialectically between, on the one hand, theories of democratic organization and revolution, and on the other, data on organizations that purport to be democratic and involved in social transformation—primarily Nicaragua's CEBs, then CEBs in El Salvador, Guatemala, and Brazil, literacy campaigns in Brazil and Nicaragua, and a civil defense committee and a farmer's association in Nicaragua. The method is qualitative, historical, and comparative.

The theoretical model's four requisites, each having structural and ideological characteristics, include independence from central authority, a means of coordination, openness of membership, and consensus as the means of decision making. Descriptive models of the various cases illustrate how the theoretical model has been executed in practice, including its limits and contradictions. The descriptive models also indicate the need to include the change agent, who organizes the community and whose position is contradictory: representing both the central authority and the community organization. The organization, in particular the change agent, is proposed as a probable link between the micro-level of the individual members and the macro-level central authorities of Church and state. When the community-based organization comes into conflict with the central authority, the change agent must often choose to whom her/his primary obligation is as representative. Prescriptive models note the limits and contradictions of the descriptive models and, based on their successes, direct how and under what circumstances the theoretical model can be more closely approximated.

This book is intended to be an aid for studying and cultivating democratic organization for social change. It should be of interest to Latin Americanists, theorists of religion and revolution, democratic organization and social change, education and community development, as well as to those who are more practically involved in these issues.

Acknowledgments

I would like to express my gratitude to the Nicaraguans; the Nuevo Instituto de Centroamerica of Cambridge, Massachusetts; the Humanities and Social Science Research Council of Canada; and to the University of California for enabling the research and writing of this book.

The names of Nicaraguan private citizens have been changed to protect their anonymity.

Democratic Organization for Social Change

1

Introduction

THE PROBLEM AND METHOD

A key problem in social change, related to local-level organization, is how to cultivate an organization based on participatory democracy which empowers its members to oppose an oppressive authority and participate in a revolutionary reconstruction of society. This study traces this process in Christian Base Communities (*Comunidades Eclesia de Base*, CEBs, or Church Based Communities) in Nicaragua, and explores as well the circumstances of constraint. In studying this problem the methods I employ are qualitative, comparative (Glaser and Strauss 1967), and historical. In so doing I follow Collins's advice by defining science as "a way of finding the common principles that transcend particular situations," seeking conditions for variations in a phenomenon, and giving "the conditions under which some things happen rather than others" (1975, 2). By studying Nicaragua's CEBs I will illustrate the common explanatory principles which enable the CEBs to function as democratic organizations engaged in social transformation, and conditions under which they fail to do so. In this introduction I will briefly discuss the method and how it developed, before turning to the definition of key terms.

In order to explain a phenomenon a theory is created. Glaser and Strauss describe the process of creating grounded theory. They argue that theory should be generated from data and not the converse. They continue that once created, the theory is then to be illustrated by characteristic examples of the data (1967, 3). Comparative analysis further qualifies the theory created from the original case, making theory generation an ongoing process; one which is not completed by the conclusion of a study (23–32).

Glaser and Strauss recommend that the researcher not approach his data with preconceived theories into which he forces his data to conform. Yet they admit that "one goes out and studies an area with a particular sociological perspective, and with a focus." Their suggested solution is to make a distinction between formal theory and substantive theory, the former informing the researcher's approach, the latter being generated from data. In this way the researcher may use pre-existent formal theories to see if they help to explain his data. And his data-generated substantive theory will help to reformulate established formal theories (33–34).

Although this approach appears more scientific than approaching data and field research with preconceived theories, it is one which fails to acknowledge all of the subtleties and difficulties in such attempts at objectivity. Among others the work of Garfinkel (1967) and Romanucci-Ross (1985) illustrate the problems of ethnomethodology, selective attention, and socialization in creating bias and inescapable subjectivity in the research process. A self-reflexive realization of one's own history and so the bias and limitations to one's approach can only strengthen objectivity as well as academic history.

In going to the field and conducting secondary research for the collection of data, I was informed by an academic history which focused on the role of religious ideology or theology in social change. This influenced both my selection of the case study as well as a theoretical predisposition to finding data which supported the importance of ideology in democratic organization and social change. In addition formal theories of organization and conflict conditioned my attention to a structural analysis of the data collected.

These theoretical predispositions, though limitations in Glaser and Strauss's method of grounded theory construction, also have benefits. Religious ideology—liberation theology—is an important element in the CEB. It has its own history and a method of study known as exegesis. It explores religious belief using scientific methods which historically situate any theology and seek to explain how various interpretations and meanings are given to religious symbols. My background in this study enables me to be familiar with and not overlook the important role ideology plays in social organization. The meaning given to religious symbols and their motivation to social continuity or change is further discussed in this chapter under "Structure and Ideology."

My method is also historical, and as such is informed by the work of Stinchcombe (1978). Like Glaser and Strauss, Stinchcombe argues that the "more detailed study of particular historical sequences" or "narratives" provide the evidence for theories. He continues that "the test of any theory of social change is its ability to analyze such narrative sequences," by paying attention to those "bits," those "narrative details" (1978, 10–14).

As such, in paying attention to bits of detail, I will be engaged in what Stinchcombe defines as a "microsociology," "the constituent human thoughts and actions . . . which make up collective or structural outcomes" (19). However, the collective and structural outcomes which make up national revolutions are macrosociology, and the relationship of micro- and macro-sociology is a problem in itself, discussed in this and the following chapter. The collective and structural outcome in this case is the CEB engaged in the revolutionary process. The bits of narrative detail are the beliefs and practices of CEB members. In my comparison of the CEBs within Nicaragua, and then with the CEBs in other Latin American countries and other organizations that purport to be democratically engaged in social transformation, I focus on individual cases and actors. This comparative method follows Stinchcombe's advice:

The comparison of structures is being built up by detailed . . . reconstruction of the actions that make up the structures, and especially the *long series of actions to differential selective pressures* that produce variant patterns of socially organized action. The molecules of these molecular processes are active humans making up their minds. (52–53)

In the reconstruction of the CEBs I look for patterns which produced democratic organization engaged in social transformation, and patterns which limited such organization. From these patterns I draw up what Stinchcombe refers to as "a model of what a [democratic organization for social transformation] should look like" (73). By model, I mean as Stinchcombe does, an "ideal type" in the sense of Weber's use of the term in reference to the Calvinist ethical pressures that give rise to capitalism (1904). Stinchcombe characterizes this application of model or ideal type to the CEBs as a "virtual choice ideal type." As such it is not so much a question of causality as it is of what similarities are present in the cases under study that account for the CEBs' development, success, and failure. In the case of our theoretical model, it "need be neither an empirically possible type nor even one which can remain for a long time stably in men's minds—it can have internal tensions either as a social structure or as a mental structure which prevent it from maintaining itself" (Stinchcombe 1978, 63–64). Rothschild and Whitt employ this method in the development of "an ideal-typical model" of collectivist and democratic organizations (1986, 50).

The model of democratic organization for social transformation which this book develops is very much this ideal type, a theoretical model. It may not even be an historical possibility due to its internal contradictions. Yet, it is a model of what a democratic organization should look like if it is to be engaged in social transformation. The analysis that leads to drawing it up includes the following three steps outlined by Stinchcombe. I use these steps also to articulate three different model types in this book.

First, the researcher extracts from the historical cases, here the CEBs and literacy campaigns, the relevant characteristics (whose relevance Stinchcombe argues, depends on the researcher's interests and theoretical bias). In describing these historical cases a "descriptive" model is created—how a democratic organization for social transformation was illustrated in the CEB, literacy campaign, or other mass organization. Second, one explicitly derives the set of characteristics that will maximize the likelihood of a democratic organization bringing about social transformation. This is the "theoretical" model or "ideal type" which provides the characteristics of democratic organization for social transformation in abstract general form. Third, the concrete historical entities, the CEBs and literacy campaigns, are "measured against this abstract maximizing ideal type and judged as pretty close or pretty far away" (Stinchcombe 1978, 73–74). Noting the limits and successes in the descriptive model and its contradictions with the theoretical model's ideal, a "prescriptive" model suggests how the particular case studied might more successfully implement the ideal type.

Through this three-step process, the resulting theoretical model provides us with a standard by which to measure organizations that claim to be democratic and engaged in social transformation. It also has the potential predictive value of indicating the likelihood of such organization and transformation occurring given the antecedent characteristics as measured by the requisites of our theoretical model.

In the first step of this analytic process, Stinchcombe points out that the relevant characteristics which the researcher extracts are influenced by the researcher's interests and theoretical bias. Thus, in this case at least, the process of model construction has not been one which sprung spontaneously from research data. Not only has this process of model construction been influenced by theoretical biases, it has also been a dialectic process moving between theory and data and back to theory again to reformulate the conditions under which democratic organization for social transformation occurs.

It was this dialectic process that indicated the need to specify an agent which was originally absent in the theoretical model. Agency is the relationship in which one person, an agent, represents another person or groups of persons, acting on their behalf (White 1985). It was the change agent who, with varying degrees of success, formulated the descriptive model in the historical cases studied. That this was not clear at the beginning of the research process and theory construction—from neither the theory review nor the description of the cases—indicates the value of the dialectic between theory and data in comparative studies. In studying the descriptive models of the various historical cases, we see how change agents—external missionaries or educators, or internal community leaders—attempted to put the theory of democratic organization for social transformation into practice. In studying their shortcomings and limitations the prescriptive model suggests how the change agent might overcome those limits based on the ideals of our theoretical model and the successes of our descriptive models.

Also, the CEB is not the revolutionary society writ small. Such a claim would lead us into unanswerable questions of causation: What part of the revolution was caused by the CEBs? This comparative historical study, drawing up a theoretical model or "ideal type . . . as a frame of reference for the historical case account," the descriptive model, follows Skocpol and Somers's advice in not pretending to generalities of causal inference to which it is not entitled (1980, 181). A national revolution is macro-level change. Yet for this macro-level change to occur, local-level organizations must empower individual participants. The CEB is one instance in which we can illustrate and study the revolutionary process in action, one descriptive model of democratic organization for social transformation. As such the "theoretical model" needs to be elaborated *"before* turning to the historical case illustration," the descriptive model, which only serves to "illustrate and clarify—and potentially, refine it" (177, 191).

The theories I will review are of social conflict and democratic and revolutionary organization. What do these theories suggest characterizes a democratic organization if it is to participate in the revolutionary reconstruction of society? My data primarily consist of field research, material from archives, as well as interviews with and observations of the CEBs and to a lesser extent other mass organizations in the Nicaraguan revolutionary process, with special attention paid to the literacy campaign and the action of the Civil Defense Committees (Comite de Defensa Civil, CDC).

The CEBs were selected as the basis for this model because they meet the criterion of having explicit participatory and democratic purposes (Rothschild and Whitt 1986, 27). Liberation theology, constitutive of the CEBs, involves the application of social science to a community to improve the life of its members. The CEB provides a case for studying this practice of ethnographic research in determining the community's needs, psychological tools in developing the member's self-esteem, and sociological knowledge in the organization and mobilization of its members for social transformation.

My previously outlined method requires dialectically moving between the research data on the CEBs and theories of democratic and revolutionary organization. I begin by drawing up a theoretical model of democratic organization for social transformation which develops out of this research, and then return to my data to see how it further qualifies the model (Glaser and Strauss 1967, 25). I will illustrate how the CEBs, popular-education campaigns, and other mass organizations fulfilled the model's requisites, how they did not, and note the circumstances under which they fell short of the ideal type model. This will increase the explanatory power of the theoretical model (3): to delineate conditions under which such requisites for democratic organization for social transformation are not maintained.

A major part of this study then presents the more systematic examination of the CEBs in terms of this ideal type model: studying their history, formation and practice, and their interface with the revolutionary process in Nicaragua. After reviewing the CEBs in Nicaragua, I will extend the comparative analysis to CEBs in El Salvador, Guatemala, and Brazil, to see how they fulfill or fall short of the requisite characteristics of democratic organization for social transformation. In order to further strengthen the power of the model, and to demonstrate its applicability beyond CEBs, I will review the literacy and popular education campaigns of Brazil and Nicaragua to see how they might further qualify the model. I will end this comparative analysis with a firsthand look at the workings of several other mass organizations in Nicaragua, to illustrate further the function as well as the limits and contradictions of our theoretical model in practice.

Finally, I will discuss the predictive value of this theoretical model and its possible applications. The study seeks to explore the possibilities of such organizations for social change and their limits; to understand how these constraints can be minimized and participatory democracy maximized; under what conditions is such a democratic organization likely to occur? To this end I suggest that the reader keep in mind that although the specific subject studied is Nicaraguan Christian Base Communities, this research is concerned with the development of democratic organizations for social transformation.

WHY THE CHRISTIAN BASE COMMUNITIES IN NICARAGUA AS SUBJECTS?

CEBs involved in the Nicaraguan revolution have been selected for study for several reasons. My subject of investigation is democratic organization for participation in a revolutionary process and as such the Nicaraguan organizations offer ready and current examples. In popular knowledge and the media many claims have been made concerning the contribution of CEBs in the revolutionary movements of Latin America. The Church traditionally has not been considered a revolutionary element or a democratic structure, therefore studying how it has purported to become both may illustrate more clearly the salient requisites in the democratization of traditionally authoritarian structures. A recent case study of CEBs in a region of El Salvador attributes the success of the revolution to the organizational work of the CEBs (Kincaid 1987).

The CEBs in Esteli were selected as prime subjects for participant observation and interviews because Esteli is a rural town in north central Nicaragua. Much smaller than Managua, it was easier to come to know in my six-month stay, it made the countryside more accessible, and the town is known in Nicaragua for how well it is organized in support of the revolution. Some exploration of the CEBs in Managua offered a variation of locale, being a large urban center, removed from the contra-Sandinista fighting that occurred in the region of Esteli.

Nicaragua was also selected because of its historical significance; a country where the revolution has triumphed (Nicaraguans refer to the revolutionary overthrow of Anastasio Somoza in 1979 as *El Triunfo*, The Triumph), the fight continues against external aggression, and where the size of the population, just over three million inhabitants, has enabled a high level of organization of the citizenry in the revolutionary process (Mulligan 1988). Nicaragua's success in local-level organization also posits the hope of the development of such exemplar organizations, not only in the revolutionary transformation of third world countries suffering under oppressive oligarchies but also in the democratic transformation of first world and second world Communist countries which have become so large and bureaucratic (Weber 1968), or single party dominated (Michels 1949), as to be no longer participatory.[1] In third world countries in particular, the Church still is a powerful institution that might challenge the existing system (Cleary 1985).

Last, my own interest as a sociologist of religion and revolution has led me to select the CEBs in Nicaragua as my prime subject for a case study of democratic organization for revolutionary participation.

DEFINING THE TERMS: REVOLUTION, DEMOCRATIC ORGANIZATION, AND CHRISTIAN BASE COMMUNITY

To begin, some terms need to be defined, namely, revolution, democratic organization, and Christian Base Community. A revolution has been distinguished from a rebellion and a coup d'etat in that neither of the latter accomplish long-term and pervasive structural changes (Skocpol 1979). Some have argued that the success of a revolution should be measured against the ideal of the nationalist socialist dream: independence from foreign domination and a more egalitarian society (Walton 1984, 209). Others propose that a revolution succeeds to the extent to which the benefits of the revolution are delivered by the social movement organizations (Gamson 1980, 1043), that is, the organizations of the revolutionary movement (McCarthy and Zald 1982).

I propose that the necessary requisite, if a revolution is to be a social transformation, is a structural change in the power base (Weber 1946, 229), empowering previously disenfranchised masses by enabling them to participate in the direction of their society. Otherwise one does not have revolution, or social transformation, but merely a social change, substituting one elite authority for another (Trimberger 1986, 171; Marx 1972; Wolf 1969).[2] For a social transformation, I propose, the revolution must provide these masses with both a structure and an ideology which enables and promotes their participation. This is done through a democratic organization. When the goal and structure of an organization are to enable its members to participate in their self-direction it may be referred to as a democratic organization (Rothschild and Whitt 1986).

In developing this model of democratic organization for social transformation I employed my case study of Nicaragua's Christian Base Communities. The roots of the CEBs precede Vatican II and their styles vary in their attempt to accompany the poor (Bruneau 1980, Levine 1981). Yet, the CEBs' coming to the forefront in Church history in Latin America is based in efforts of the Second Vatican Council (1962–65) to modernize the Catholic Church and address social problems, the recommendations of the Latin American bishops' Council of Medellín (1968) that urged the Church to make "a preferential option for the poor" and the Council of Puebla (1979), which referred to the CEBs as the "hope of the Church" (Cleary 1985). These communities or CEBs, as they came to be known, are grass-roots organizations to evangelize, educate, and organize the poor so that their spiritual and material needs could be better met (Gremillion 1976; Bamat 1983, 219; Dodson and Montgomery 1982).[3] Although coinciding with parish boundaries, CEB members are more oft than not a highly motivated participating core of the parish. At times they were formed by the recruitment and training of these members by the priest, or in the case of the diocese of Esteli, Nicaragua, under the direction of the bishop. At other times they were formed by missionary religious, or Delegates of the Word who are lay persons and community leaders, trained by religious to form such community-based organizations. At other times—especially recently with the active opposition of Cardinal Obando y Bravo, CEBs have been formed in parishes without the support of the local priest or even against his wishes. Although CEBs flourish in Protestant Evangelical Churches as well, our focus here will be with the Catholic Church, encompassing the vast majority of the Nicaraguan population.

When the CEBs were proposed at Medellín and again by the Latin American Episcopal Council at Puebla, it seemed apparent that their intent was to provide community-based opposition as a part of the structural solution to the institutionalized poverty of Latin America. In Nicaragua this was apparent to the dictator Somoza, who, because of the activity of the CEBs, banned the use of the word *comunidade* (community) and destroyed one of the first model CEBs in Nicaragua on the island of Solentiname in Lake Nicaragua, established by a priest, Padre Ernesto Cardenal, who became Nicaragua's Minister of Culture under the Sandinistas. (Dodson and Montgomery 1982, 172). The CEBs' self-defined goals were to involve the participation of the laity in the direction of their Church, the critical analysis of their society, and in active participation in meeting their community's needs (Vega 1977). The CEBs are therefore democratic organizations as defined above.

STRUCTURE AND IDEOLOGY

The problem given is how to cultivate an organization based on participatory democracy which empowers its members to oppose an oppressive authority and participate in a reconstruction of society in which participatory democracy remains characteristic of the organization. Various theorists have laid out general necessary structural conditions. Although they have referred to the importance of ideological requisites, these have been less critically studied (Zald 1980, 65). Ideology, being more problematic, warrants further discussion.

In any ideology the interpretation given to a myth and the meaning given to a symbol is of importance. So too with the meaning given to the Christ symbol, considered as ultimate authority in the Christian belief system. As social scientists we study the varying ideologies of liberation theology as opposed to the traditional scholastic theology in order to determine their motivational effect on believers. In doing so as ethnographers, we use the terminology of believers, whether theologian, religious, or lay participant, in an attempt to describe "in terms consistent with the discrimination made by the [believers] themselves" (Metzger and Williams 1963, 407). As in Garfinkel's studies in ethnomethodology (1967), we must attempt to don the hat of those we study.

Using the religious terms of analysis of various believers, as Lan did in his study of popular religious belief, "when sources are biased in a consistent way, we are in fact offered the opportunity to study the workings of the popular mind" (1985, 14). This parallels Stinchcombe's historical method. Therefore, ideology, in this case religious ideology is constituent to structural outcomes and must be studied and understood in the language of the common believer and analyzed for its meaning and motivational impact.

In this study we come to find that liberation theologians, Catholic as well as Protestant religious working closely in CEBs, and CEB participants hold, in general, a common explanation of the reason for the suffering of the poor in Latin America. Their analysis is centered in an ideology which sees this suffering as a result of structural inequities. They also see this injustice as an opportunity to organize as a community of believers in a struggle to better the lot of the poor and so achieve what they perceive as justice—a measure of God's Kingdom on Earth. In contrast, the ideology of the Catholic Church hierarchy, as expressed by various conservative bishops, and in the words of traditional scholastic theology, has a great deal in common with the belief statements of Protestant Pentecostals, whether in El Salvador, Guatemala, or Brazil. Both consistently preach salvation as an individual matter, noninvolvement in politics, and the maintenance of the social order by support of traditional political and Church authorities. In their belief system, progress towards the Kingdom of God, only to be achieved in the life to come, could be forwarded by individual work habits and acts of piety.

This is not to negate the variety in CEB styles and membership. Studies have demonstrated a variety—including the more conservative and devotional. Similarly, progressive, community oriented Pentecostals exist (Bruneau 1974, 1982; Mainwaring 1981). The intention of this simplification is not to present these groups and ideologies as homogeneous, but rather to present an ideal type. Donning the 'hat of the social scientist, we now attempt to explain religious ideologies in terms consistent with the belief of scientific ideologies, in this case concerning motivation and collective behavior. Geertz classically defines religion as

a system of symbols which acts to establish powerful, pervasive and long-lasting moods and motivations in men by formulating conceptions of a general order of existence and clothing these conceptions with such an aura of factuality that the moods and motivations seem uniquely realistic. (1972, 168)

Theologians and social scientists of religion alike have recognized the importance of the meaning attached to religious symbols (Berger 1967). If, as Tillich claims, one's belief system or religion is the expression of one's ultimate concern in life (1957), then the meaning attached to religious symbols is of vital importance in providing a vision of how life should be and values which orient believers' activities towards accomplishing that vision (Baum 1972). Religious ideology, theology, as an orientation of one's values and behavior, cannot be ignored by social science in understanding social change.

Among others, sociologist Bellah views religious institutions as one of, if not the only, organizational force which can counter the trends in the predominantly secular society (Bellah et al. 1985). Mannheim has spoken of religion as a revolutionary force involving a change of meaning associated with the religious symbol (1936).

The meaning attached to a symbol will convey the "organizational value set" of the religion, that is, the legitimate discourse and activity for believers (Neuhouser 1989, 234). Neuhouser attributes the radicalization of the Catholic Church in Latin America in part to the experience of the oppression of poverty and in part to a change in the organizational value set, or meaning given to that experience in Vatican II, Medellín, and liberation theology (1989, 234–38). The political nature of liberation theology, its challenge to the status quo of the existing economic and political order, and the traditional legitimating role of that order played by the Church, is admitted by liberation theologians (Planas 1989).

Other studies have illustrated the role of religious ideology in support of revolution, and have sought to understand and convey the point of view of the religious believers. As with the CEBs, Renato Constantino's work on popular religious movements in the Philippines, presents these movements as "genuine vehicles for the expression of the people's dream of national liberation and economic amelioration" (Ileto 1979, 10). The question raised is how do believers, participants in these religious movements, "actually perceive, in terms of their own experience, the ideas of nationalism and revolution?" (5).

In the following chapters I will attempt to follow the solution suggested by Fields in *Revival and Rebellion in Colonial Africa;* that is, "more adequate description of the participant's belief and practices" (1985, 22). I will endeavor, as Lan does in *Guns and Rain: Guerrillas and Spirit Mediums in Zimbabwe* (1985), to draw out the salient features from the commonly expressed beliefs and experiences of the CEB members interviewed in order to explore the basic concepts out of which their political/religious ideology is constructed.

We will examine the importance of the varying interpretations given to the Christ symbol in the traditional scholastic theology and the theology of liberation as expressed in the words of CEB participants. The realization of the political implications of this ideological concern was not just made by theologians. It was also recognized by the ultraright advisors of Ronald Reagan before his ascendency to the presidency, as expressed in the Santa Fe document:

The United States should take the ideological initiative . . . the war is to conquer the consciousness of humanity. The ideological-political element will prevail. . . . The political extension of the United States should begin to confront (and not simply react afterward) the theology of liberation as it is used in Latin America by the clerics of the theology of liberation. The role of the Church in Latin America is vital for the concept of political liberty. [In so far as] political liberty is expressed in private property and productive capitalism and whatever other concept is less Christian than communist. (Hynds 1980, 1)

The interference of the United States in Latin American churches is not new. It is well documented by Hynds who reports the Central Intelligence Agency (CIA) funding of conservative church groups and their influence in national politics. Returning from a visit to Latin America in 1969, Nelson Rockefeller spoke of "the threat of the conclusions of Medellín" where the Church was called to assume "a preferential option for the poor" and how that made the Latin American Church vulnerable to a "subversive penetration" (1980, 2).

In accord with Brazilian educator Paulo Freire, as education cannot be free of politics, liberation theologians have claimed that neither can religion. "Education is never neutral. Left to itself, conventional education socializes students into the values and worldview of oppressors" (Cleary 1985, 76); so too with religion. Our concern here is primarily with the question of dif-

fering religious ideologies and the orientation of activities that they promote. A traditional scholastic theology of much, but not all of the Church
hierarchy projects the Old Testament image of the suffering servant as the
interpretation of Christ, and in contrast the liberation theology of the CEBs
projects the Old Testament image of the liberating warrior, bearer of justice, as the meaning given to the Christ symbol.

Padre Carlos, an Argentine worker priest,[4] involved in the CEB movement and interviewed in Esteli, provides us with a theological description
of the difference in ideology between the liberation theology of the CEB
movement and the traditional scholastic theology of the Catholic Church
hierarchy and their political interface.

Liberation theology, the Christian Base Community, the popular Church are the
same reality, and it's not an accident that it came out of the experience of Latin
America. My ecclesiastical studies, a half a year in Buenos Aires and philosophical
theology in Rome, was a traditional, a European theology developed in the First
World. Therefore it is passivist, since the seminaries were peaceful. It doesn't question. It isn't really concerned with the real world because in that reality nothing
happened. It is not based in the reality of Latin America. . . . In the years of the
1950s, '60s and '70s I integrated this theology with my experience of the working
class . . . for the first time we mixed with the poor . . . were no longer bourgeois
. . . in a context of direct contact and a reality of the dependence of an underdeveloped country. . . . A moment came when we saw that Argentina is a poor
country but has one of the most fertile capacities of all the countries in the world.
. . . We discovered it was an historical lie to say Latin America is a poor country
when it is one of the most potentially richest places in the world. . . . And yet we
see our children die of starvation. They are all malnourished. Therefore as Christians we must compare the historical, political, economic and social reality with our
biblical faith and here the problem begins. A God of the passive Europeans can't
be the God of my reality. It doesn't serve me and can't be the God of the Bible.
God calls Moses as a leader of those oppressed since he hears the cries and needs of
the people. The people of Latin America have been crying for five hundred years,
since the first Christians came to "help" Latin America. If one believes in this God
He isn't going to come in magic. But liberation theology is a reinterpretation of
Christian thought which we learned was no longer serving us. Therefore with the
same bible but different realities we come to different conclusions—a God who is
not passive, but cares. God who is bothered by the Latin American reality: children
dying of hunger. Therefore I'm not neutral because I love politics more than I hate
it; since the reality of the monastery is beautiful, but what reality is that? Not Latin
America's. . . . We are reclaiming this idea of Christ as liberator of the poor and
oppressed. . . . But when I compare this image to that of the traditional scholastic
European theology of John Paul II there is no comparison. (Journal Entry 73, 8
July 1985)

The motivating force then behind the ideology of liberation theology was
the experience of a structure of oppression. Similarly, the type of analysis,

either Marxist or developmentalist, which is given to the socioeconomic situation by those who conduct the *cursillos* (courses) for CEB formation, is also an ideological question. The symbols that are attached to a people's religious faith and the meaning given to them provides believers with their interpretation of reality (Tillich 1957; Baum 1972). It is a question of the sociology of knowledge: In the socialization process, how do people come to know, to interpret the reality in which they exist (Garfinkel 1967; Sahlins 1976)? Whether the traditional scholastic theological image of Christ as the suffering servant provides a meaning for sacrifice and suffering in this earthly life for a heavenly reward after death, or a liberation theology's challenge to work to create the Kingdom of God on this Earth by struggling against oppression and for justice, either interpretation is precisely that—an interpretation. These differing theologies employ alternative sociological interpretations. The socioeconomic analyses of Latin American poverty which accompany these theological interpretations, respectively a developmental theory of progress or a Marxist theory of class conflict and exploitation, are also theories, interpretations which purport to provide explanations of the reality suffered by the Latin American poor.

Both theologies have a social context. One has its origin in the privileged position of clerics in the paternalistic monarchies of Europe's Middle Ages, and the other, in the experience of religious whose education in contemporary social sciences assists them in their analysis of the poverty of Latin America—a reality which they share with their parishioners. The experiences of those different contexts provides differing interpretations. On one hand, as Rosa, a CEB participant, testifies, it was through the cursillos that, "For the first time I came to see something that the bishops never told us; that the land belongs to those who work it and when the poor believe in the poor we can construct the Kingdom of God." On the other hand a non-CEB participant exclaimed with excitement while waiting for the openly antirevolution and anti-CEB Cardinal Obando y Bravo's visit to the cathedral in Esteli, "The Word of God is coming to visit us." Both are interpretations of experiences that religious symbols have imbued with meaning, providing an orientation for believers' lives. Is one more true or more real than the other? That is not the job of social science to judge, if that judgment can be made, but we can study their origins and how these beliefs articulate with the believer's organized behavior. So, our problem remains, "Through what combination of ideology and organization" does a revolution empower the masses to participate in their self-direction? (Himmelstein and Kimmel 1984, 1154)

2

Constructing the Model

REVIEWING THEORIES OF REVOLUTION AND DEMOCRATIC ORGANIZATION

Salert argues that revolution requires a structural change (1976). Various Latin American social scientists (Freire 1973; Le Boterf 1981; Jara Holiday 1981; Vilas 1982; Arroyo and Medina 1982) argue this structural change transforms the power base by providing organizations in which the masses, who, previously had been illiterate and disenfranchised, can participate in the direction of their society.

Students of the Nicaraguan revolution have argued that "to 'test' a revolution for democratic tendencies, the place to begin is by analyzing how far it gives rise to autonomous mass organizations representing majority interests and how such organizations mediate between the new institutions of state and civil society" (Coraggio and Irvin 1985, 24). The revolution then, in the case of Nicaragua, would have to be defined as an ongoing process of change (Collins 1986, 1), *el proceso revolucionario* (Coraggio 1985, 106), "based on what Nicaraguans call 'the logic of the majority'" (Collins 1986, 2). Former Nicaraguan Foreign Minister Padre Miguel D'Escoto defined the revolutionary process as not static but rather as subscribing to a democratic ideal with aspirations to a system of social justice. It is therefore a process of creating a democratic system that involves all the people, not just the elite. Indeed, usurpation of revolutions—won with the blood of the masses—by an elite group has long been recognized (Marx 1972, 436–525; Wolf 1986). Elite revolution limits mass participation in politics and preserves social and economic inequality (Trimberger 1986, 171).

In contrast to elite revolutions, empowering individuals so as to insure mass democratic participation requires more than an ideology which calls for their participation. It requires structures, organizations in which they can participate. Coraggio, an Argentine social scientist and director of research at the *Coordinadora Regional de Investigaciones Economicas y Sociales* (CRIES) in Managua, defines this critical requisite.

But the crucial political element is the systematic search and implementation of ways to make it possible for the people, increasingly organized and autonomous, to convert themselves into the revolutionary subject, losing as such the conditions of "the masses," of the anonymous and automated citizen. (Coraggio 1985, 16)

This lies at the root of the notion of popular power, a power of the masses which developed through the process of revolution against the Anastasio Somoza dictatorship, and which necessitated organization of opposition (1985, 78).

A debate has developed in the sociology of conflict, most notably between Gamson and Goldstone, over the definition and measurement of the success of a revolution: whether to consider "partial advantages" as successes or failures (Goldstone 1980, 1020). This debate will be addressed in this study only in so far as the revolutionary organizations studied fulfill the requisites of our ideal type model of democratic organization for social transformation.

THE PROPOSED SOLUTION: DEMOCRATIC ORGANIZATION FOR SOCIAL TRANSFORMATION

I propose that a revolution defined as a process which empowers people must provide them with a structure and an ideology which enables and promotes their participation, that is, with democratic organizations. In theory, such a democratic organization would be structured so as to enable its members to organize for critical analysis of their social problems and to mobilize to obtain solutions to them. A constitutive part of such a democratic organization would be an ideology of self-worth and self-determination which supports participation in self-direction. We need to examine not only how the democratic organization cultivates ongoing individual participation in the revolutionary process, but also, first, how it creates an organized opposition to the prerevolutionary system.

THE CHRISTIAN BASE COMMUNITIES AS SECONDARY ORGANIZATIONS

Tilly has argued that for a revolution to occur, the revolutionary movement must be part of at least a minimally organized group with resources (1978). Various sociology of conflict theorists (Michels 1949; Lipset 1956;

Oberschall 1973; Pinard 1971) have advocated the necessity of secondary organizations to provide a basis for opposition to the central authority or government. Secondary organizations are social-movement organizations which participate in the revolutionary process by mobilizing opposition to the established order. They are "secondary" because they are not part and parcel of the established order. If they were part of the established institutions they would be limited in their ability to express opposition to the status quo of which they are an integral part. With regards to our case, the traditional hierarchical Catholic Church structure is part of the established order, whereas the CEBs are secondary organizations.

The CEB, as a secondary organization, would also provide its participants with the tactical mobility, that is, the ability to mobilize resources, which Wolf argues is necessary for the successful outcome of peasant revolts (1986, 173). Kincaid's study of peasant rebellions in El Salvador puts the successful outcome of the revolution in the area of Aquilares squarely on the shoulders of the community organizational work of the CEBs. Once formed, the CEBs there "began to address problems of land tenure, employment and social justice—pitting peasants against estate owners and local security forces," and drawing the community, now organized around its problems, inextricably into rebellion (1987, 484, 490).

Michels (1949) first studied the tendency for authoritarianism to develop, even in "democratic" and postrevolutionary societies, where such secondary organizations were absent. Lipset (1956) developed this thesis by proposing that Communist regimes tend to become authoritarian because of the absence of secondary organizations which are independent of and have the ability to criticize the central authority. Michels pointed out that secondary organizations provide the base for opposition to the central authority only under certain conditions, most notably where they are free of authoritarian control and able to mobilize in opposition (1962, 401). Lipset claimed that independence from the central authority is a necessary prerequisite for effective opposition, as are the unique historical antecedents which allow the opposition to flourish (Lipset, Trow, and Coleman, 1956, 17), and in the case of revolution, succeed in overthrowing the central authority. For our concern, in order to prevent domination by an unheeding central authority, it is of equal importance, for the maintenance of the revolutionary process, that after the overthrow of the pre-existing regime, the secondary organizations maintain a separate identity from the new central authority.

Also necessary for the success of a revolution is a host of antecedent conditions; economic and political, as well as those specific social ones we will be considering. Many of these are external, that is, beyond the control of the revolutionary organization, and so also beyond the scope of this study. These conditions are, of course, of great importance in determining the outcome of the revolution and range from world market forces and local poverty to how widespread community rebellions are, the weakened condition of the ruling elite or state apparatus that has lost support of influential groups, the presence of an opposition group ready to take over state control, and the importance of external allies. Kincaid's study points out, referring to the work of Skocpol and Tilly, "social revolutions are highly unlikely to succeed where dominant class unity and the coercive apparatus of the state remain largely intact" (1987, 466, 490–91). I will refer to these antecedent external conditions only in so far as they affect the local organization, in micro-level interactions.

SITUATING THIS STUDY: MACRO- AND MICRO-LEVELS OF ANALYSIS; PROVIDING A CONTEXT AND ARTICULATING THE INDIVIDUAL'S EXPERIENCE

The problem of linking macro- and micro-levels of analysis is a prominent one in social science. How do we relate a description of CEB members' participation in the revolution to revolutionary antecedents created by Nicaragua's place in the world capitalist system (Wallerstein 1979), the resulting shifting modes of production (Taylor 1983), and the economic and political oppression of Nicaraguans? Various theorists have treated this problem differently, depending on their theoretical approach. To the macro-level sociologists, approaching the problem from above, the micro-level local interactions are presented as a determined outcome, often of economic forces.

Walton argues that underdevelopment may be linked to revolution as increased unrest corresponds with increased economic and political deprivation (1984). More specifically, in terms of our individual unit of analysis, world market forces resulted in the "semi-proletarianization" of the Nicaraguan *campesino* (peasant farmer) (DeJanvry and Garranon 1977; Biderman 1983, 8). Changing modes of production—the large scale commercialization of agriculture, the expansion of agro-industrial estates exporting cash crops, in particular coffee and cotton—forced the campesino off of subsistence plots of land and into the underemployment of seasonal wage labor, or into the sprawling new urban slums in search of employment (Paige 1985, 1975). This loss of land, and so of a livelihood, was supported by the state apparatus, controlled by the large landholders, export enclaves, multinational corporations that benefited from the trade, and foreign governments, in this case, the United States and its military aid.

To micro-level theorists, often anthropologists, looking from below, the macro-level social change is generally expressed in terms of how it is experienced by individual participants and local communities. From this perspective the macro-level change is analyzed in so far as it affects the individual and local community; seeking to convey the participant's belief system in coping with this change on the local level.

My approach to this macro-micro problem is informed by the work of

Knorr-Cetina and Cicourel, and the theory of Habermas. In their work Knorr-Cetina and Cicourel (1981) use the macro-level to provide a context for local-level interaction. I too will seek to link this macro-level context with the micro-level individual discontent which found expression and organized opposition through the experience of CEB participants. My approach, being micro-level, will focus on the experience of the individual CEB member.

The CEB member, however, participates in an organization with selected local, regional, and national representation, therefore involving macro-level coordination. Habermas refers to organizations as mediators between macro- and micro-levels of analysis. He argues that new organizations, responding to strains on the macro-level, provide the people thus organized with a learning experience which contains a moral element. Habermas proposes that the learning capacities, first acquired by individuals in marginal groups, become adopted by nonmarginal members of society and so are used to reorganize action systems, and thus eventually the macro-level. He thus proposes a model of social change which integrates macro- and micro-levels, using the organization as an intermediary level:

The solution that I would like to propose is as follows; the species is able to *learn* not only in the domain of technical knowledge—a domain decisive for the growth of productive forces—but also in the domain of moral-practical awareness that governs the development of structures of interaction. (1981, 259–68)

Habermas provides us here with a suggestion which this work will attempt to execute: analyze the organizational level in social change both structurally and ideologically.

I will not attempt to solve the problem of integrating macro- and micro-levels of analysis here. In so far as it is addressed, however, it will be done from the organizational perspective and to some extent from below, that is from the micro-level of the experience of the individuals. Such an attempt at linking macro- and micro-levels of analysis from below, as far as possible using the individual's experience as the unit of analysis, suffers from all of the difficulties of ethnography (Garfinkel 1967; Romanucci-Ross 1985). Though it may not express the complexity of the world capitalist system, this approach at least attempts to communicate the effect of that system on the individual most marginalized, most traumatically affected by its workings.

It is in their words and their analysis that we will come to see the effect of world market forces, of the loss of their land to expanding large landholdings cultivating luxury export crops, and their attempt to regain power in their lives in the face of oppressive state or hierarchical apparatus. As one former campesino and CEB participant testified:

On their farms they [campesinos] were paid poorly for their harvest, and they would become indebted when the harvest failed. They [large producers] would monopolize, corner their [the campesino] land. And merchants sold for so much more. Therefore there was oppression. For example, a merchant would buy for five cordobas and then sold for ten cordobas. When a campesino took loans, they couldn't pay back. (Journal Entry 386, 5 September 1985)

This, and other factors, such as the repressive actions of the state (Skocpol 1979), the frustration of the new industrial bourgeois (Roxborough 1979) with the Somoza dictatorship's monopolization in the case of Nicaragua (Biderman 1983, 29), heightened by the economic crisis of the 1970s and the fall of world market prices for Nicaragua's cash crops (Booth 1982, 175), provide the context for the CEBs.

Following Habermas' advice, by focusing on the organizational level I also attempt to illustrate a meeting point, an intermediary level of analysis at which those most abused by the system attempt to influence its effects on them by organized actions. The work of a CEB in the outskirts of San Salvador provides an example. Attempting to buy some land for a housing co-op, one member stated the problem in finding an affordable tract. "It's nice and cheap, but it's so far away that we'll have to pay four times as much on the bus—and then the women who take in washing or sell tortillas in the urban districts, what are they going to do? No, it won't work." The missionary religious working in this CEB, on hearing this, provides our micro-level perspective with a participant's analysis from below of macro-level forces as they experience them.

I understood why San Salvador is ringed with slums, shacks piled one on top of another with such horrible living conditions. They are all people who have come from the interior looking for work. The coffee harvest only lasts two months a year. The same goes for cotton and sugar. What about the rest of the year—all those months of battling hunger and sickness? So the people come to the capital to work on construction gangs or whatever they can find. (Galdamez 1986, 31)

However, taking the organization as our unit of analysis has its own problems. Examining the coordination of local CEBs, whether city-wide, as in the cases of Esteli and Managua, regionally or nationally, raises the question of how these various levels articulate with each other and the role the change agent plays in this coordination. Can full democratic participation characterize the organization when selected representation is required for interorganizational coordination? Is this selected representation by leaders not then once removed from the local level and full democratic participation? How do the CEBs then relate to the national revolution? These questions illustrate the problem of the micro-macro link. Such regional and national coordination is necessary if the revolutionary movements are to succeed. Such coordination, however, requires a method of select representation which precludes the full democratic participation of all members. This is an inherent limitation and fundamental contradiction in our model and of democracy in practice. This limitation will be elaborated further in the development of our model.

SOME STRUCTURAL CHARACTERISTICS OF A DEMOCRATIC ORGANIZATION

In turning to this theoretical model or ideal type, let us first look at some of its characteristics as delineated by various theorists. With all the criticism of bureaucracy and of revolutions and their often repressive aftermaths, are the CEBs or any organizations able to meet up to the ideal of operating democratically? Michels is pessimistic concerning the ability of an organization to maintain functioning on democratic principles as it expands. "He who says organization, says oligarchy" (1962, 365). Michels, however, is making his generalization to all organizations based on political parties whose object is to expand political power (Rothschild and Whitt 1986, 23). I propose that Michel's "Iron Law of Oligarchy" can be qualified and the democratic tendency maintained in organizations if two elements are provided: a structure which guarantees and requires the participation of all members, and an ideology which not only calls for full democratic participation, but which makes the organizations's objective to serve the needs of its participants.

Concerning the structural requisites, Gamson argues that a strong leader, and so the tendency for authoritarianism, can be avoided to the extent to which participants are familiar with the processes of the organization (1975). Knowing what needs to be done, members can participate fully in their self-direction; they need not depend on a directing authority who holds some elite but necessary knowledge, either procedural or concerning the subject to be addressed. Weber argues that under certain conditions, such as small size and functional simplicity, an organization can avoid structures of domination and maintain democratic forms (1968, 289–90).

SOME IDEOLOGICAL CHARACTERISTICS OF A DEMOCRATIC ORGANIZATION

Weber refers to a fourth basis of legitimation of authority, that of "value-rationality" (1946, 229). I refer to this guiding ethic as an ideological requisite to avoid authoritarianism and maintain democratic participation. Elaborating on value-rationality, where Weber did not, Rothschild and Whitt argue that cooperative or collectivist organizations remain democratic because "they are committed first and foremost to substantive goals, such as peace, equality and good health, to an ethic, even where this overrides commitment to a particular organizational setting" (1986, 22). In the case of the

CEBs the principal value-rationality or guiding ethic is that the organization is to serve the needs of the community as determined by the CEB members. I propose that this ideological commitment to service and to participatory democracy is as necessary as the structure in empowering members to democratic participation, and in avoiding authoritarian domination. "Here authority rests not with the individual, whether on the basis of incumbency in office or expertise, but resides in the collectivity" (51).

Though general structural conditions necessary for revolutionary organization are laid out by various theorists, the necessary ideological conditions are less critically studied. Oberschall points to the importance of the ideological element in the analysis of social conflict and of social movements. He quotes McClosky's definition of ideology as a "system of belief that is elaborate, integrated, more or less coherent, which justifies the exercise of power, explains and judges historical events, identifies political right and wrong, and furnishes guides for action" (1973, 178). The ideology of CEB participants would be expressed in their belief system. Ideology, defined in these terms, addresses the same concept as Weber's value-rationality as a means of legitimation. Ideology is equally employed as a means of legitimation for revolutionary participation. The necessity of ideology in revolution is clearly and emphatically stated by Crane Briton: "Ideas are always part of the pre-revolutionary situation . . . no ideas, no revolution" (Oberschall 1973, 178).

Rothschild and Whitt, in their study of democratic collectivist organizations, list several characteristics which would come under our ideological requisites of democratic organization for revolutionary participation. Foremost, again, is the idea that authority resides in the collectivity, to be arrived at by consensus (1986, 50–52). This illustrates the integrated nature of structure and ideology in the reality of the life of the organization. Consensus in decision making would be the structural means of executing the idea that authority is to come from the collectivity itself. The opinion of each participant would be necessarily solicited and discussed by the group in arriving at its collective decision. I will separate the structural and ideological elements of democratic organization for social transformation for the sake of analysis. I will refer again to this correlative nature of structure and ideology in the description of our model.

Rothschild and Whitt appear to argue for the predominance of ideological characteristics over structural ones for the functioning of a democratic organization. Ethics, they propose, are prominent, with rules being minimal. Furthermore, social control is based on moralistic appeals, and social relations on the ideal of community. Even recruitment is largely of friends with shared sociopolitical values. Thus, solidarity and normative incentives are primary, material incentives secondary (if existent), advancement is meaningless and the resulting structure is nonhierarchical and egalitarian (1986, 52–64).

Having reviewed some of the theoretical literature on democratic organizations and organization for revolutionary participation, let us explore what the resulting model of democratic organization engaged in social transformation looks like.

3

A Model of Democratic Organization for Social Transformation

THE METHOD REVIEWED

I have proposed to provide a theoretical model of democratic organization for revolutionary participation, as I have proceeded above, based in part on reviewing the sociological literature on democratic organization and secondary organizations. The other part is based on data collected through field research—participant observation, interviews, archival material including historical surveys and guidelines for the formation of the CEBs. In answering how the CEBs fulfill the characteristics of both a democratic and a revolutionary organization, that is, one engaged in social transformation, a descriptive model is provided. Studying the conditions under which it falls short of the theoretical model provides the basis for the prescriptive model. By comparing how the CEB activities vary in our case study, in other Latin American countries, and how democratic organization is attempted in education campaigns and other mass organizations, I employ an historical, qualitative, and comparative scientific methodology in order to generalize from the particular situations. I look for conditions of variation in these particular situations or cases in order to arrive at common explanatory principles. In this way I hope to contribute to the identification of some of the salient features required and so construct a theoretical model of an organization that is both democratic and revolutionary rather than a mere description of the structural and ideological form they take in any one case. Studying the particular form such organization takes in the case of the CEBs, however, illustrates the possibilities as well as the limitations in constructing a democratic organization for social transformation. Furthermore, it is possible for an organization to be democratic and not engaged in social transformation or revolution. In the cases studied here the democratic organization is developing in an historically undemocratic context and so is socially transforming by its very attempt to practice democracy in such a context. In this sense our model is of a democratic and revolutionary organization.

So constructed, what does our model look like? Generally stated, such a democratic and revolutionary organization must provide a structure which enables the group to organize so as to participate in the formation of the revolutionary society and have an ideology which provides the group with a vision of that new society which guides their participation. Based on the definition of a revolution as a transformation which enables broad based participation in direction of the society, and moving between the theory presented and the data collected, this model of a democratic and revolutionary organization can be fleshed out by proposing certain structural and ideological characteristics as necessary correlatives for the revolutionary process. They are diagrammed below so as to indicate the dialectic and mutually constitutive nature of structure and ideology.

One might argue that ideology preceded structure, since the CEBs were constructed as a response to new Church doctrine (Berryman 1984), drawing on the traditional religiosity of members (Kincaid 1987, 492). On the other hand, as we shall see in our historical overview of the CEBs, it was the structural condition of local religious living with the poor and knowing their oppression that brought about change in Church doctrine and a call to create structures which would empower participants, such as the CEBs (Bonpane 1985). At any rate, it was the oppressive structure of poverty and the concentration of power and wealth in the hands of a few to which the ideology of liberation responded. And it was through the structural organization of the CEBs, built on community bonds (Kincaid 1987, 490), that the members were able to express their concerns in a united way so as to confront the oppressive structure and participate in changing it. Our historical case study will indicate how intrinsically interwoven the two are.

A MODEL OF CONTRADICTIONS

Presented in this model are four general characteristics. The more obvious contradictions appear between the first two, though some exist as well between the third and fourth characteristics. I suggest that this contradictory nature creates a necessary tension through whose dialectic a democratic organization and revolutionary process is able to exist in a largely authoritarian society.

This theoretical contradiction is illustrated in our descriptive models—of a CEB and literacy campaign. However, the description of the case studies and the dialectic between that data and our theory indicated a need to qualify our theoretical model to include a mediation, an agency. In the cases studied this agent of change embodied these contradictions. The change agent is the party responsible for forming the democratic organization and engaging it in social transformation. Yet the agent is characteristically a representative of the central authority—Church hierarchy or government—or mediator between that authority and the organization.

This agent in most of our cases was an individual, or individuals. Typically, the catalyst for change was a missionary religious organizing a CEB or an educator organizing a literacy study group. On occasion that agency was the community itself organizing for change. Even in the latter case, however, differentiation based on talent resulted in group leaders who acted as principal agents.

The diagramatic presentation of our theoretical model separates predominantly macro- from micro-level requisites for the sake of analysis, though in reality these characteristics overlap (see diagram of "A Model of Democratic Organization for Social Change"). The agent is represented. Prior to the organization itself becoming the agency of change, the change agent would be an individual or group which introduces the organization into a community. The agent's position between requisites with contradictory characteristics indicates the tensions inherent in the agency of democratic organization for social transformation. It is important to keep in mind that we are discussing not only how an organization is democratic, but also how it is revolutionary in opposing a pre-existent central authority.

What follows is a discussion of this model as related to the theories reviewed above.

A THEORETICAL DISCUSSION OF THE MODEL'S CHARACTERISTICS

Authority

Our first characteristic concerns relation to authority; structurally a freedom from central and external authority and ideologically a recognition of the right to self-determination with authority residing in the collectivity. In Weber's understanding of it, having authority meant being able to command in such a way that those commanded felt obligated to obey (1968, 946). Michels has claimed that opposition organizations must be structured as secondary organizations (Michels 1962, 401; Lipset, Trow, and Coleman 1956, 80), independent of the central authority and external control so that they can freely criticize the existing system. In our case this entails CEB independence from the Church hierarchy and state control—both the Anastasio Somoza dictatorship and the Sandinista government.

To sustain such a structure, Rothschild and Whitt propose that members must subscribe to an ideology supporting it, namely that authority resides in the collectivity which has a right to self-determination (1986, 51). In the

A Model of Democratic Organization for Social Change

Structural Requisite		Ideological Concomitance
M	1. Authority	
a	↑	
c Independence from central		The right to self-determination
r and external authority	Agent	with authority residing in
o	↑	the residing in the collective
-		
l	2. Coordination	
e		
v A means of coordinating		Recognition of interdependence
e local organizations and		and need for coordination
l input to central authority		
M	3. Openness	
i	↑	
c Open membership and		Recognized self-worth of each
r opportunity for meeting	Agent	individual and their rights
o	↑	
-		
l	4. Consensus	
e		
v Consensual means of		Egalitarian belief in
e soliciting and addressing		self-direction by full
l members' needs		participation of membership

revolutionary process the democratic organization must be able to maintain this freedom from central and external control as well as avoid authoritarianism within its own ranks, where one leader of an elite group dominates the organization.

Coordination

Our second pair of concomitant characteristics concerns coordination among similar organizations and with the central authority, which could be the state and in our case is also the traditional hierarchical Church authority. Coraggio and Irvin have recognized the need to coordinate local mobilizing organizations if a revolution is to succeed (1985, 24). Wolf refers to the need for "tactical mobility," as a freedom from the control of the oppressive central authority, if the opposition organizations are to mobilize resources successfully (1986, 173). Coordination is needed both in overthrowing the previous central authority as well as in working with the new revolutionary central authority in meeting the needs of the individual organizations as well as the revolutionary society at large. It would involve a CEB's coordination with other CEBs and their relationships with other revolutionary organizations, including the revolutionary vanguard, the *Frente Sandinista de Liberacion Nacional* (National Sandinista Liberation Front, FSLN), and after the revolutionary triumph, with the state, the Sandinista government. A concomitant ideology with emphasizes community solidarity in our model organization is all the more important when the organizational work must be done in the context of "a strong trend toward declining village autonomy" (Kincaid 1987, 491).

Although this second characteristic, the need for coordination, appears to be in contradiction with the first, the need for freedom from authority, the contradiction is one of several which we will be examining in our data. It results in a tension which, I will argue, in the last instance, is not resolved, but is necessary for the functioning of democratic organizations in the revolutionary process.

Openness

Our third characteristic of openness addresses the need for a democratic organization to be open to all who wish to participate if it is to be representative and empowering. It also requires a means by which meetings are often and easily accessible so that members can have their concerns addressed as they arise. At first this appears to contradict Rothschild and Whitt's description of recruitment in democratic organizations based on friendship and shared social values (1986, 55–56). Can opposition be expressed if membership is that personal and selective? Can such an organization as a CEB empower members of a community if membership is only open to those with shared beliefs? Although we will bring our field data to bear on this question, Gamson hints at a partial solution which the multiplicity of mass organizations in the Nicaraguan revolution bears out, that is, the pluralism of organizations (1975, 130–43). While one might not join a CEB, for example, because one does not share its religious beliefs, one could join a neighborhood Evangelical Protestant organization or a secular organization such as a Civil Defense Committee. This also counters the danger of seeing collective behavior (Gamson 1975, 130) or communities as homogeneous or in isolation. There is rather internal differentiation and also penetration by national political and, in this case, religious structures (Kincaid 1987, 466–94). Ideologically, this openness of membership requires a "value-rationality" as means of legitimation (Weber 1946, 229). This ideological concomitant promotes the recognition of the self-worth of each individual, their opinion, their rights, and the organization's commitment to be at the service of the community, guided by an ethic of meeting the basic needs of each individual (Rothschild and Whitt 1986, 22). In this manner the organization strives to meet the revolutionary goal of recognizing the dignity of each individual and ending the condition of the anonymous masses (Coraggio 1985, 16).

Consensus

The fourth characteristic, consensus, as with the others, contains the contradictions and limitations of human organization: striving for perfect democratic participation when organizations are internally differentiated according to the individual differences and assets of each member (Rothschild and Whitt 1986, 70). If consensus is to be an effective means of organization, the group size must be small. Jean-Jacques Rousseau wrote that participatory democracy would only work in groups where "each citizen can with ease know all the rest" (Rothschild and Whitt 1986, 92). Recent empirical work supports this proposition (22). This is a narrow definition of participatory democracy. For this study, and more conventionally, democracy denotes soliciting the input of all participants at the local level. This would require select representation. Organizational tiers in larger geographical meetings for the sake of coordination—the town as opposed to the neighborhood, regional and national groups—would require selected representation. Even within the base, organization meetings will be lead by individuals identified and selected because of their leadership abilities (Kincaid 1987, 483). Different people have different talents and skills and in the dynamics of the group certain leaders will come forward (Duberman 1972, 37). Representation must be responsible, accurately representing the consensus of one's constituents.

Therefore there is again the necessity of a concomitant egalitarian ideology in which self-direction through the participation of all members is valued. This would guard against dominance of the group by certain individuals. Structurally then there must be a means of soliciting from the members what each considers to be important and needing redress. This in turn would require skills of social analysis as well as communication and dialogue skills, ranging from self-esteem to learning to listen, if a true consensus is to be arrived at. It also requires the demystification of knowledge, both procedural and of the subject matter (Braverman 1974), so that all members can fully participate and leadership roles can be rotated (Rothschild and Whitt 1986, 104–14). This would counter specialization in the division of labor, which Weber maintains as the primary source of bureaucracy (1968). Thus Weber proposed that it is only under the conditions of small size and functional simplicity that an organization can remain democratic and avoid structures of domination (1968, 289–90). Nevertheless, as I have argued, responsible representation allows for extended size.

THE DATA

This model of structural and ideological requisites for a democratic organization, if it is to be revolutionary, suggests what the student of such an organization should and should not find. Are the CEBs one instance of such a democratic and revolutionary organization? In studying the role of the CEBs in the revolution in El Salvador, Kincaid concludes that "a closer look at the concrete, local-level interactions . . . could only strengthen the analysis, and these interactions constitute a major avenue for further development of this topic" (1987, 490). It is this local-level interaction which my data and analysis will seek to address. How does the CEB create community solidarity and the requisite conditions for the successful participation of a democratic organization in the revolutionary process?

I propose to begin with an historical review of the CEBs and then to examine the survey data on their development, relationship to the established Church and Somoza dictatorship, and guidebooks for their formation, in order to seek out their ideological and structural characteristics. Details, idiosyncrasies, and contradictions from participant observation and interviews will be included to illustrate how the CEBs fulfill and fall short of the requisites of the model. After studying the CEBs in El Salvador, Guatemala, and Brazil, I will then review the adult literacy campaigns, Civil Defense Committee, and a farmers' organization for structural and ideological parallels, again supplementing the illustration with observations from field research.

The other three Latin American countries were selected in order to study the effect on the CEBs of varying conditions of relation to the central authority of state and Church hierarchy. In Nicaragua's case opposition by state was replaced by support of the state and opposition of the hierarchy after the revolutionary triumph. In El Salvador there has been continued repression by the state and support from the hierarchy. The CEBs in Guatemala have suffered the repressive actions of the state and opposition of the hierarchy, whereas in Brazil the hierarchy has been supportive and the state much less repressive.

Through this historical, qualitative, and comparative methodology, I intend to provide some of the general characteristics necessary for local-level democratic and revolutionary organization, how they are executed in a particular case, and some of the conditions under which these requisites are not met and the consequences. This will contribute to the predictive value of analyzing the structural and ideological components of an organization with regard to its meeting its projected revolutionary goals.

4

Nicaraguan Christian Base Communities

BACKGROUND TO THE CHRISTIAN BASE COMMUNITIES

The Nicaraguan CEBs share a common history with CEBs throughout Latin America. The roots of the CEBs of Latin America lay in the context of poverty and oppression and also in the directives and theology of Vatican II, a Roman Catholic Church Council held largely for the purpose of up-dating and making relevant its traditional theology to meet the needs of modern peoples, or, as stated by the Council itself, "reading the signs of the times" (Gremillion 1976, 12). "Above all, the emphasis on identifying the church with the poor led to the assumption of a more prophetic attitude toward society and politics." Although this prophetic attitude always ex-isted in Scripture and theology, it is central to the theology of liberation which "interpreted the gospels' demanding that Christians be a force ac-tively working to liberate the great majority from poverty and oppression" (Dodson and Montgomery 1982, 162; Gutierrez 1973; Boff 1979; Segundo 1973). "The theology of liberation grew most fundamentally out of the Church's direct involvement with the working poor, both urban and rural. . . . Direct involvement was a profoundly unsettling experience of con-sciousness-raising" (Dodson 1979, 206).

This theme was of central importance at the Medellín (1968) and Puebla (1979) conferences of the bishops of Latin America, whose countries are predominantly Catholic and poor. They claimed that the Church should make "a preferential option for the poor" (Bamat 1983, 219). From their experience—juxtaposing poverty to their Christian belief, revitalized by Vatican II—came the call for justice, an end to first world economic exploitation of the third world, and, more particular to our concern, the setting up of Christian communities, grass-roots organizations. These organizations were to evangelize, educate, and organize the poor, who more often had been ignored by the Church, so that their spiritual and material needs could be better met. Thus it was that CEBs came into being in many Latin American countries under various names (Dodson and Montgomery 1982, 162, 179; Bruneau 1980; Levine 1980).

Because the CEBs were grass-roots innovations they tended to vary from diocese to diocese in their name and in their precursors (Cleary 1985, 113). At times they grew out of pre–Vatican II movements aimed at involving the laity, such as the Family of God or Catholic Action. At other times they grew out of the cursillos[5] or manuals for CEB formation, animated by Medellín; those by José Marins being the most famous. At first they were often merely referred to as *comunidade*, in other places as the Church of the Poor or the Popular Church. Carrying out on a practical level the suggestions of Vatican II, Medellín, Puebla, and liberation theology, the CEBs' major objectives included "instruction in depth, direct use of the bible, a sense of community, new ministries, the emergence and empowerment of the laity, and emphasis on working at the side of the poor" (109). "Community leaders are the key to the continuity and dynamism of the communities" (113). As with the communities themselves, the leaders' titles and functions vary, from *presidente* and *responsable* to *dirigente*, though the most commonly used was *delegado*, from the Delegate of the Word movement.

National pastoral meetings of Latin American priests in 1968 and 1971 discussed how to implement Medellín and Vatican II. "At this meeting [1971] they concluded that evangelization had to be aimed at conscientizing" (Dodson and Montgomery 1982, 164).[6] National organizations of priests urged that "the priest must analyze the society in which he works, determine where the chain of exploitation begins, and denounce publicly the social and political relationships which are found to lie at the root of exploitation" (Dodson 1979, 207). Thus, in establishing the CEB, often the priest would be the agent of change. Both structurally and ideologically he, or the lay leader, the Delegate of the Word, would be caught in a contradiction between the Church hierarchy—the centralized authority—and the community he was directed to serve and empower.

In Venezuela, as early as the 1960s, as an answer to the call of Vatican II, *Los Cursillos de Capacitacion Social* (Courses or Seminars for Social Empowering, CCS) were formed as a Catholic response to the alleged Communist infiltration in universities. Although originally anti-Communist, the CCS "sought the objective of Christian revolution in Latin America." The cursillos were developed throughout Central America by Jesuit and Maryknoll fathers and sisters, "working very closely with university and high school students. . . . Subjects included God and science, the Church, Christian morality, the family and modern social problems, the social doctrine of the Church and university action" (Bonpane 1983, 12–13). One such predominant social doctrine was the traditional hierarchical teaching of the right of workers to organize. Pope Paul VI's encyclical *Populorum Progressio* (1967) went so far as to imply when a revolution would be just: "We know, however, that a revolutionary uprising—save where there is manifest, long-standing tyranny which would do great damage to fundamental personal rights and dangerous harm to the common good of the country—produces new injustices, throws more elements out of balance and brings on new disasters" (Bonpane 1980, 184). In this and additional famous statements by Pope Paul VI such as, "No one has the right to keep for himself what he does not need when others lack basic necessities," and, "If you want peace, struggle for justice," the traditionally conservative Vatican hierarchy seemed to provide encouragement for action for social change (*Populorum Progressio*, 1967). Pope Paul VI also provided an impetus for university students to act: "It belongs to laymen, without waiting passively for orders and directives, to take the initiative freely and infuse a Christian spirit in the mentality, customs, laws and structures of the community in which they live" (Bonpane 1980, 184).

The CEBs claim to be democratic organizations engaged in social transformation by responding in part to these teachings and those of liberation theologians, in part to the critical social analysis of the Latin American situation which rejected developmentalism, and, most importantly, to the oppressive poverty and political repression in which they struggled to survive daily. In further exploring their history in Nicaragua and my particular case studies, a descriptive model will be provided, examining how they fulfilled each of the four requisites of our theoretical model for such an organization.

AUTHORITY

What was the relationship of the CEBs to central authority? With regards to the hierarchical Church there was practically no relation. Because of this they were able to act as secondary organizations, free of the central authority's control, in this case the traditional, hierarchical Church structure. For the latter this was more true in Nicaragua than in Brazil where the creation of the CEBs was encouraged by the Church hierarchy. The Catholic Press Association of the United States further verified the hierarchy's lack of control of the Church, particularly in rural areas, profiling hierarchical directed services of the Nicaraguan Church at the time as "virtually absent in the countryside where more than half of the Nicaraguan people lived" (Dodson and Montgomery, 1982, 162).

That the CEBs were free of the hierarchy's control in Nicaragua is indicated from a dialogue held between the laity and hierarchy in 1977, two years before the revolutionary triumph, in which the hierarchy investigated the origins and purpose of the various lay organizations throughout the country. An unpublished archival document, this hierarchy-laity dialogue showed that the bishops had little contact with or knowledge of the Church in the countryside, with the exception of the bishops of Esteli and Blue-fields (Vega 1977). This investigation of the CEBs, and of two movements involved in establishing CEBs, the Delegates of the Word and *cursillos de cristiandad*, also indicates the ideological commitment of these Nicaraguan grass-roots organizations as they defined themselves. They called for greater dialogue with and support from the episcopate and for greater interest in the struggles of the politically oppressed and poor for economic and social justice. The CEBs suggest a pastoral renovation which "gives priority to pastoral work in rural campesino areas . . . and to marginal sectors in general," and that "the option for the poor should be more definite" (Vega 1977, 17–18). The CEBs describe themselves as "the small nuclei that act as a catalyst," "seeking fraternity," and employing a "methodology [of] analysis of the concrete" "social and economic necessities of the small community," "forming the critical consciousness of its members," "in order to seek a solution" (Vega 1977, 13, 24). The CEBs in their self-evaluation in the same document refer to their primary obstacle as the political repression of the Anastasio Somoza dictatorship (40). Indeed many Delegates of the Word, lay persons trained to establish CEBs, were reported killed for their organizing activity (Dodson and Montgomery 1982, 171–72).

Even towards the end of the Somoza dictatorship the hierarchy of the Church in Nicaragua could still be characterized as mediators and moderates, opposed to Somoza, but fearing a Sandinista victory (Van Vugt 1985, 6). The Church centered in the CEBs, which came to exist throughout Nicaragua, however, "became revolutionary in the years between 1972–79 by virtue of coming to identify Christian liberation of their people with the armed struggle led by the Sandinista Front of National Liberation" (Dodson and Montgomery 1982, 162). The distancing from the hierarchy and the growing revolutionary involvement as secondary organizations can be illustrated by two precursors of the CEBs, the Delegates of the Word and CEPA.

The Jesuits in Nicaragua, with their hierarchy's support, had founded the Center for Agricultural Development and Advancement (CEPA) in 1969 "for the purpose of training peasant leaders to organize politically their own communities." "CEPA was created originally as a self-help program designed to meet their daily needs more effectively. In time, these efforts came to center on organization as it became clear to CEPA members that peasants could not improve their conditions without organized collective political action" (Dodson and Montgomery 1982, 170). Thus it was that the Church provided the first organization of agrarian laborers under Somoza.

Similarly, by 1975, the Capuchin Fathers had trained 900 Delegates of the Word in the department of Zelaya, which was entirely rural and the largest department in Nicaragua, comprising much of the eastern half of the country. "After Medellín, the Capuchins encouraged the selection and training of Delegates in the Christian Base Communities. The delegates were trained to develop the Christian formation of peasants, focusing on literacy, conscientization and health. Religious services themselves consisted of dialogue based on biblical texts and focused on pressing needs in the life of the community." The Delegates, as in all CEBs, employing this methodology, took "the teachings of Medellín which formed part of their training, and developed them in an explicitly political direction [focusing] on social issues" (Dodson and Montgomery 1982, 171, 164).

Like the Delegates in the CEBs, the CEPAs "integrated political demands, such as the right to land, as sanctioned by the Christian gospel" (Dodson and Montgomery 1982, 170). Realizing that political action was necessary to obtain these demands and the hostility of *Somocismo* to the peasants, the Delegates of the Word often became politicized and militant, which invited persecution from the *Guardia Nacional* (National Guard), and resulted in the death and disappearance of CEPA members where it was strongest. The Sandinistas, in turn, had become more open to the Christian bases for political action. It was not until 1977 that the FSLN created their own Association of Rural Workers (ATC), and then "some key CEPA workers joined the ATC and became directors of the organization. Other CEPA members joined the FSLN as armed combatants and at least four CEPA workers were killed by the National Guard during this period of increased radicalization" (Dodson and Montgomery 1982, 170).

The hierarchy attempted to restrict the political activities of CEPAs at this point, but the CEPAs declared themselves independent of the hierarchy—as the CCS had earlier in Guatemala—considering themselves "to be doing religious work, occasionally in cooperation with the FSLN" (170). But by this time the CEPAs had a broad grass-roots base of support. Correspondingly, the Capuchin Order realized with the persecution of the Delegates of the Word "that there was a political basis for Guard repression" (170–71). But unlike hierarchical superiors whom we will study in the Guatemala case, the Capuchins made the decision in Nicaragua to come out publicly against the regime because of the rapidly polarizing situation (170–71). So it was that on these two occasions, the agents of change, Jesuit and Capuchin religious, intermediaries between the micro-level communities and the macro-level Church hierarchy and state, caught up in the contradiction of being representatives of the community-based organization and the central authority, threw in their lot with the community.

Not only were the CEBs free of central authority and critical of it, but they also mobilized resources to challenge the dictatorship. My case study of the history of the CEBs in Esteli offer an illustration of both of these aspects. As Padre Philipe, a local native priest, explained, in Esteli the CEBs grew out of the further organization of natural communities that were first organized in assemblies, "to join people together to do service . . . who can help whom?" The lay-trained Delegate of the Word would coordinate the CEB for catechetical instruction and social service. The cursillos were "the first form of motivating the laity to be active in the Church." Before this organizational work, Padre Philipe characterized the Church in the diocese of Esteli as "very traditional and passive." He claims that young religious—himself included—reformed by Vatican II and Medellín were motivated to confront the problem of "social economics" and "military repression" in their countries. Padre Philipe's own experience provides an example.

In my first parish there was a coffee production plant. The owners of this coffee factory and those who brought their coffee there, the small producers, related in such a way that the owner of the factory would buy the coffee production of the year, prior to the harvest, and charge interest on it [the loan]. This impoverished the campesino [small producer]. And there was military repression, the military command of Somoza here who had houses of prostitution. . . . Each prostitute paid taxes to the military. . . . This affected my pastoral conduct. I wrote a letter to the boss of the Esteli military security, since I saw the campesino tortured, and I published it in the newspaper. . . . How could I defend them? To join them together they are stronger. Therefore to protect their lives I arranged the CEBs in the diocese of Esteli. (Journal Entry 844, 27 October 1985)

At first the CEBs were established under the directives of a sympathetic bishop who hired Padre Philipe to be pastoral regional coordinator of the CEBs in 1976. Padre Philipe went on to explain the reaction of Somoza, the secular authority, to the organized resistance:

Somoza accused six priests. I wasn't included. One North American was expelled, and the others, Nicaraguans, continued here with difficulty and were detained for some time. And this is how the practice of this sort began. The people were full of fear and they could speak only in one place, the church. . . . For example, a person disappeared, we would try every form to find him or her, public demonstrations. They killed one boy. They put electric cords down his nostrils into his stomach and shocked him to death. We in the church organized to release the body and to defend the family. Thus the first form was to organize by manzana and by blocks [a manzana containing six blocks]. Thus the Civil Defense Committees were born in Esteli. In each manzana, if someone was captured, they would handle it within the manzana and blocks. In this manner they would organize for defense. But they could meet in the church. Therefore people of different manzana met in the church and established good relations. Afterwards this was for political and military organizing, but now we don't need that part, but rather to motivate and support, and this is how the Civil Defense Committee was formed in Esteli. (Journal Entry 844, 27 October 1985)

We see here that not only did the CEBs act as secondary organizations, free of and critical of the central authority and engaged in mobilizing resistance, they also served as the model and base of the Civil Defense Committees, post-Triumph secular organizations that parallel the work of the CEBs and serve as the neighborhood militia. Acting as secondary organizations the CEBs appeared to be an integral part of *El Triunfo* (Dodson and Montgomery 1982, 162–77).

After the revolutionary triumph, the independence of the CEBs was further verified during my stay in Nicaragua in 1985, as the reactionary Cardinal Obando y Bravo described the CEBs as "works of the devil," and yet their membership continued to flourish and grow. To whip up support for himself and his anti-Sandinista position, the previously distant cardinal became very interested in his country and travelled extensively, visiting dioceses during my stay.

When he came to visit the cathedral in Esteli I asked Don Pedro, my host, father of the primary subject family for my study, and a leader of his barrio's CEB, if he would go to see the cardinal. He answered, "No. He may be a man of God but his politics are rotten." Furthermore, in the diocese of Esteli, the CEBs had been cultivated originally at the direction of the local bishop, who hired a priest for that express task, Padre Philipe. After the revolutionary triumph and the new directives of the cardinal, the bishop withdrew his support. The local CEBs, however, with the assistance of missionary religious free of the bishop's control formed their own headquarters, *Instituto para Formacion Permanente* (Institute for Permanent Christian Formation, INSFOP), and continued to expand into the countryside forming new CEBs.

In one instance in the parish of Fatima, when the bishop ordered the church closed because of the involvement of its missionary priest and pastor, Padre José, in the CEBs, the active core of the parish, strongly involved in the CEBs, retained the keys to the church and said that it was theirs to open and close. They continue to support Padre José, a Belgian missionary, who still celebrates at his church with his parishioners, even though the bishop has ordered him to leave. A refugee from El Salvador, Padre José explained to me that the bishop had written to Belgium asking the bishop there to recall him, but that it was the head of his order who had that authority. When I asked, "And if the head of your order recalls you?" he responded, "I will not go. The people here are the ones who give me authority and I will stay as long as they want me" (Journal Entry 612, 8 October 1985). Padre Philipe provides another example of a change agent whose representation of the community was primary when it came into conflict with his role as representative of the central authority. We can see the struggle and tension involved in the democratic organization's attempt to maintain independence from a central authority, particularly in the case of the CEBs, historically situated within a traditional hierarchical Catholic Church where authority is passed down from the top of the hierarchy, the episcopate. We also observe that the CEB is not only revolutionary for the laity, but empowers the participating religious as well, investing them with a new authority from below.

The continued support of the CEBs for the revolution and their vital importance in some towns is illustrated in the case of La Trinidad. A small town of 500 inhabitants on the Panamerican Highway, just seven miles south of Esteli, it is known for its hospital, one of Nicaragua's primary ones, and also for a pastry shop, one of Nicaragua's finest. At the north end of the town is a government-owned grain storage bin, a part of the government's efforts to insure distribution of basic crops (beans, corn, and rice) throughout the countryside. The name for the town derived not only from the Christian belief in the Trinity, but also because it is surrounded on three sides by tall cliffs, making it an easy target for bombardment from the plains above. Estelianos are open about La Trinidad's former reputation as a base of support for Somoza, and its continuing conservative nature after the Triumph.

During my stay in Esteli, a band of contras attacked La Trinidad as part of a major offensive which had encircled Esteli in an attempt to get a base in the region. Shelling the town, they succeeded in hitting the hospital, destroying the grain storage bin, holding a busload of foreign Evangelicals hostage for a short time, and in Llano Largo, a smaller town on the plain above, destroying the *expendio* or government-supported food store and the school. Speculation in Esteli was that they attacked La Trinidad hoping to find some support there in the previously pro-Somoza town.

Arriving in La Trinidad the day after the attack, I interviewed members of the CEB and Padre Philipe. In my interview of CEB members they emphasized that they were also members of the CDC, trained in maintaining watch in the town for contra attacks. They also explained that it was through their participation in the CEB, organized by Padre Philipe, that they eventually came to be members of the CDC. It was the CDC which warned the townspeople of the contra attack, and when the contras came into the town, those interviewed claimed they came asking for Padre Philipe. Padre Philipe later showed me his hidden shortwave radio, which he had used to contact the Sandinista military to let them know of the contra attack.

These accounts of Padre José and Padre Philipe's CEBs in Esteli and La Trinidad are vivid illustrations of the CEB as a secondary organization, free of hierarchical control and in support of the revolution. However, the above also could be an account of how a group of laity had been indoctrinated by their parish priest to support a revolution. It does not tell us how the participants of the CEB were recruited or how they came to learn the skills of dialogue and consensus, and self-esteem—if they did. All of which are requisites of our model for full participation in a democratic organization engaged in social transformation. For this we turn to the third and fourth characteristics of our model, openness and consensus, and how they were executed as depicted in the guidebooks used in establishing the CEBs and interviews with participants. I shall return to the second requisite characteristic of our model, coordination, after reviewing the establishment and functioning of the CEBs.

OPENNESS AND CONSENSUS

With regards to our model's characteristics of openness and consensus, perhaps they can best be reviewed by recounting how the CEBs were formed. As aforementioned, missionary or local religious, often under the directives of their bishops, and inspired by Vatican II and Medellín, went out to establish CEBs within their parishes or mission district, or, due to the lack of religious, they trained local lay leaders, Delegates of the Word, to carry out this task. The CEBs were established, not as a rival structure to the pre-existing parish, but parish members who wished to study and deepen their faith were invited to join a group in reflection on the Bible. It was hoped in this way that the grass-roots organizations would be a means of revitalizing the Church and reaching out to those most neglected by the traditional Church: the rural and urban poor.

Initially, members were invited to these evenings of Bible study by other CEB members or a founding religious or Delegate of the Word, passing *casa por casa*, door to door, and getting acquainted. Once together in one person's home, a group of eight to twelve adults, who knew each other as neighbors, would break their usual conversation and gossip when the leader called for them to begin. After reading a passage from Scripture, the leader would invite the participants to share what this meant for them in terms of what they were experiencing in their lives today. In my observations that could vary from matters of the recent contra attacks to how to support a woman in the neighborhood whose husband was beating her. The leader would invite everyone in the group to participate, drawing out those who tended to hang back. After about forty-five minutes to an hour of such discussion, moving back and forth between their concerns in life and the Scripture reading, the meeting would end by establishing a date for their next meeting; the leader encouraged participants to bring new people including teenagers, to the group. Closing with a song and breaking up as it had begun—neighbors talking in small groups of two or three about their family concerns, or local gossip, or telling jokes—the group would gradually disperse returning to their own homes. If the initiate showed continued interest in attending these Bible study groups, they would be invited to attend a cursillo.

Organized by missionary religious, local priests or lay trained Delegates of the Word, the members of the CEBs refer to their attendance at a cursillo de cristiandad as their point of entry into the CEB. The cursillos are described as more reflection on their faith for the purpose of establishing a comunidade. One CEB leader in Esteli, Juan, explained that before the Triumph "we were 'community,' nothing else. The *comunidade eclesia de base* came after the Triumph. The [CEB] movement began with the movement of the Delegates of the Word, the cursillos and retreats, these three" (Journal Entry 740, 21 October 1985). These cursillos were not held regularly, but rather when there seemed to be enough new members interested and religious and lay leaders trained and available to lead them. After the Triumph the cursillos were principally practiced by the CEBs. They would be held in a location where the participants would spend two to three days together, sleeping over. The guidebooks of the cursillos provided me with further detail on these meetings, as none were held during my six-month stay in Esteli; the intense fighting given as the reason. That may very well have been the case since the retreat center established in Condega, in the countryside just north of Esteli and owned by the CEBs, was attacked and shot up by contras during my stay. The lay leaders of the CEBs in Esteli, referred me to the guidebooks of the cursillos, written by Latin American theologians, particularly Marins, as a primary tool for the weekend seminars in training new CEB members. Studying the text, along with interviews with past participants and observations, provided me with the following data on how the cursillos aimed at developing self-esteem and dialogue and consensus skills among participants.

Besides the study of social encyclicals, Church history Scripture, documents of Vatican II, Medellín and Puebla, the cursillos cultivated the democratic organization engaged in social transformation by explicitly applying the insights of social science, psychology, sociology, and anthropology, in teaching dialogue and listening skills through exercises, a political and religious history of the country, and a socioeconomic analysis of the participants' living situation.

The guidebooks apply the theology of liberation to a "this" world reality. The motivating force then behind the ideology of liberation theology was the experience of a structure of poverty and oppression. The guidebooks for the cursillos and the establishing of CEBs themselves mention their purpose as "a means to study and focus on the problems of man today in order to find a truthful solution that is Christian." "To improve life . . . through piety, study and action" (Marin 1963, 27, 29–35). It analyzes the elements of action as "intellectual reflection . . . voluntary decision and constancy . . . actualizing and diligence . . . and prayer and sacrifice." The structural means for CEB formation the guidebook describes as "methods for action:" "1. make friends," and "2. look for them and meet with them." The organizational importance is emphasized as it describes the means of "perseverance through meetings in groups" (Marin 1963, 230, 232, 261). The guidebooks themselves "sum up the fruits of the *cursillos de cristiandad* in . . . better consciousness of one's responsibility and a more clear sense of distributive justice . . . more security in one's decisions" (Secretariado Diocesano Ciudad Real 1961, 153).

Formation through the CEB seminars includes studying Church history: primitive Church community, the persecution, beginning of social integration, Reformation and Counter-Reformation, the effect of "bourgeois society" on the Church, and the concepts of community and society and how the Church is a "reserve of solidarity," a community "like the community of Exodus" (Hungs 1982, 30). Church documents that deal with subjects such as distributive justice and a just revolution are studied and discussed within the context of the participants' lives.

More important for the analysis of our model is the emphasis on development of the necessary skills of dialogue, learning to value everyone's opinion, and seeing things from a perspective other than one's own. The guidebooks explicitly refer to the importance of "the sociological and psychological aspects," "developing a conscisousness of community in faith," and "the risk of faith and confrontation with religious indifference." A guidebook in the formation of CEB members describes itself as attempting to counter the problem of "modern intelligence," that is, a nonapplied "theoretical knowledge" (Hungs 1982, 101–5).

In attempting to apply this theoretical knowledge of sociology and psychology in the creation of community the cursillos include "dialogue exercises," referred to as "Silence and Speaking." Observing and participating in a dialogue, participants analyze their and others' participation in the dialogue. Carefully planned, the exercises are given time constraints for the completion of each part. One such exercise, "Dialogue and Participation in Speaking and in Silence," is scheduled to last one hour and thirty-five minutes. The facilitator or leader of the exercise gives ten minutes of introduction by explaining the concepts and "conveying the sense of the exercise."

How do we dialogue? How do we participate in the discussion without dominating it? One can participate by speaking and not participate by speaking. One can participate by listening and not participate by listening. (Marins 1972, 108)

The facilitator goes on to explain:

There is nothing more difficult to know than how to dialogue maintaining a prudent equilibrium between the diverse forces that call on our attention. To search for the points of contact between persons and ideas without sacrificing their truth; to listen without interrupting; with sympathy, serenity, to respect the other because he/she is a person of value like ourselves, who has dignity and their own riches to offer. (108–9)

The facilitator continues, introducing the exercise by describing the qualities of a good dialogue as "clarity and intelligibility," "courtesy," "trust

. . . as much in the value of an appropriate word as in the disposition on the part of the listener to receive it," and "prudence . . . take into account the psychological and moral conditions of what you hear" (1972, 108).

The guidelines instruct that there are to be eight participants; four are to participate by listening and four by speaking. Five minutes are given to organizing these groups. During twenty minutes the four that speak try to answer questions such as the following: "What qualities and values do you admire most in a woman? The same in a man, a youth, a religious, bishop, priest, father of a family, children, brothers, etc? Analyze a particular personality, such as the pope, the president, etc."

Following the answering, in the second part of the exercise, for ten minutes, the four who have listened meet to prepare "feedback" for the four that dialogued. They are instructed to present their observations in a form such as: "I have the impression that . . . I had the sensation of listening to him in order to say." They are instructed to indicate the impression in the form of questioning, not to act as a judge such as saying, "You are a dictator," rather, "You give me the impression of acting *here and now* dictatorially because of this and that." The facilitator is to explain,

No one can refuse someone's impression because their impression is theirs. This impression doesn't reveal, nor does it judge, nor generalize. Don't say "You are aggressive," rather that you gave the impression of acting in such a mode . . . not always, rather here and now. No one judges the life of a person, rather one indicates what happened in a determined moment of his/her life, in what he/she has observed. . . . No one criticizes the content of the realized discussion, rather the comportment of its participants. (108–9)

This oral analysis is to last for fifteen minutes, then the group that got the feedback is to dialogue with those who listened; they can question and give explanations for fifteen minutes.

The third part of the exercise, for ten minutes, is an evaluation in smaller groups of the exercise, looking for personal, group, and leadership lessons that have been learned. They then gather together the evaluation that was made in the groups, and in closing the exercise the facilitator has ten minutes to comment on the benefits of the work and make clarifications if any are needed.

This dialectic or dialogic pattern is repeated throughout the exercises of the cursillo or training seminar and in the meetings of the CEBs. The larger group breaks into smaller groups for discussion, every member is asked to contribute, characteristic of consensus building, the fourth requisite of our model. If there is some material to study they are all asked to give their analysis of the material. There is a reporting back to the larger group and a criticism of the presentations and an evaluation of the benefits gained from the exercise. As we have just seen, there is an attempt to see things from the perspective of the other person in the dialogue, to put one's self in another person's role.

This recognition of the value of the other person, of their opinion and of their rights, is illustrated further in an exercise called "Classes." This is an example of the third requisite of our model, openness. An exercise lasting five hours and fifty-five minutes, it follows a similar format in that the feeling of the exercise is introduced by the facilitator; to understand the perspective of differing social classes. Breaking into groups paralleling the different social classes, for two hours a group will study materials which deal with the history and development of a particular class. The groups then meeting together would present their class in summation, an exposition followed by questions and answers. Following that a critique of each class is done by special teams composed of one member from each group, less the group that is presenting their class. This process of forming the new groups for "the evaluation of each class" and the presentation of the criticism is to last two hours and forty minutes. Again the exercise concludes with the participants reporting on all of the benefits they gathered from the exercise together as a group or individually. It is typically ended by the facilitator giving a brief summation of the results of the evaluations they have made (149–50).

This type of attempt at understanding history and getting a grasp on the different forces involved in society is characteristic of the CEBs and the mass education campaigns studied. Its effect is to make the participants informed social actors who are conscious of making history by their actions. As the mother of my host family commented on her participation in the CEB's cursillo, "It was through this that we became aware of something that we had never heard before from the bishops, that the earth belongs to those who work it. That when the poor believe in the poor we can construct the Kingdom of God" (Journal Entry 412, 5 August 1985).

Such exercises also sensitize and develop empathy for other members of society and can foster social cohesion as well as mobilize for conflict. My case study of the history of the CEBs in Esteli offers an illustration of both of these aspects. Padre Philipe's aforementioned account testifies that the CEBs grow out of the organizational need for mutual support, "who can help whom." But this "first form of motivating the laity to be active," in a formerly "very traditional and passive" Church, resulted in confronting the problems of "social economics" and "military repression" (Journal Entry 844, 28 October 1985).

At first, as mentioned, the CEBs were established under the directives of a sympathetic bishop who hired Padre Philipe to be pastoral regional coordinator of the CEBs in 1976. CEB members often had a history of earlier involvement in Church groups, such as the assemblies which Padre Philipe referred to or in the case of Don Pedro, my host, the Family of God. The leaders of the CEBs which I observed, however, not only tended to be traditional community leaders but tended to come from the middle class: owners of a gas station, a boardinghouse, a government store, a beauty salon, manager of a factory. These also provided intellectual leadership and were indicative of the success of the cursillos in creating empathy for the poorest and oppressed. They indicate that for the success of the CEB, the agent of change, in this case the middle-class leadership, must be a representative of the concerns of the marginalized and lower-class community, whom he is working to organize. This aforementioned responsible representation prevents the revolution from being taken over by an elite (Michels 1949; Trimberger 1986) or a middle class (Marx 1972; Wolf 1969).

The Barredas, an upper-middle-class Esteliano couple, are illustrative of this. Volunteering through the CEB and CDC to help with the coffee harvest, they were captured and killed by the contras in 1983–84. In an interview with their son, Luis, he described them in the 1960s as "traditional Christians." "Around 1975 or earlier they worked in the cursillo movement, completely, and so also began to work with the Sandinista front." I asked how participating in the cursillos had affected his parents. He explained how "in and of themselves" the cursillos did not recommend working in the Frente.

In the cursillos the area they have to go deeper into is the Christian aspect, but this creates a consciousness of the situation of the repression of the dictator under which we were living. . . . If I am a person not oppressed, but well off, but my brother is oppressed and I realize this is not how it should be, then I realize that I should do something so that this person is no longer in that position. If I am aware that this person is being oppressed, then I have to personally look for a way to improve the situation for them. (Journal Entry 346, 30 August 1985)

The cursillos and formation in the CEBs sensitized participants, including religious and lay middle-class members, to the plight of the poor and oppressed, their values and their perspective. However, this was not done without ideological guidance. All of the lay persons interviewed spoke of a shift in the Church and in their understanding of the Church as a result of studying and reflecting on their sociopolitical situation and Scripture in the light of the documents of Vatican II, the Latin American Bishops conferences of Medellín and Puebla, and papal encyclicals on social justice. As a result of reflecting on these directives and the analysis of their country's situation carried on in the CEBs, Juan, a Shell gas-station owner and a leader in Esteli's CEBs revealed:

People started to realize that being Christian was being concerned with how to change an unjust structure for a just structure; for example, the poor and children living in the streets. (Journal Entry 740, 21 October 1985)

Ignacio, a former laborer who has worked his way up to manager in a local factory, referred to the social encyclicals of the Church and the cursillos as a turning point in his understanding and practice:

My first experience of knowledge of my faith and Christianity was through a cursillo . . . in Managua in 1965, twenty years ago. . . . It awoke in me a clarification of the content of my faith . . . it planted in me the socio-political problem of the country, *el compromiso cristiano* [Christian obligation] in this situation; for justice in the face of these social problems. It was not radical or revolutionary, but rather a question of, "How can we change this dictatorship and oppression?" (Journal Entry 620, 10 October 1985)

Maria, an owner of a boardinghouse, speaks of the CEBs as growing out of a mutual support group:

We would meet to discuss problems of the suffering mothers [whose sons had been killed in fighting Somoza's National Guard]. . . . We got together, the group of mothers . . . through the cursillos. . . . We arrived there blind, without knowing anything. As Christians, we came to know the revolution. They spoke only of conversion, from old to new person, but that is revolution of the person. Also people came to know Church Based Community and gave an account to the unity of man, for the same man. That to be a Christian is not just to carry a bible under your arm, but to serve also; to give more, service, love, unity. Comprehension is the same. And through this we arrived at complete service; how a Christian is committed to the preferential option for the poor. (Journal Entry 659, 21 September 1985)

She spoke of the social analysis that came out of the cursillos and the work of the CEBs, concerning new "blind" recruits:

They are working but they do not know why and for whom; these are important. . . . It is like man exploiting man. You give them food, clothes and medicine, but they are tied to that place. It is more important for them to know why and for whom they are working. (Journal Entry 659, 21 September 1985)

Again, as in the experience of the Barredas, Juan pointed out the effect of participation in the cursillos on the wealthier middle-class participants like himself and the formation of community with the oppressed. His following testimony illustrates not only how the cursillos and the CEBs provided motivation and the organizational basis for mobilization of resources to confront the problem of oppression, but also brings up for question the role of the middle-class leadership. The role of middle-class leadership has long been criticized by social science; for merely using the working class as cannon fodder to achieve their own self-interested ends (Marx 1972; Wolf 1969). Need that leadership interfere with the fourth consensual characteristic in our model, an egalitarian means of self-direction?

When I began with the cursillos, we began by having meetings. We would begin by asking questions. In time we asked, "Why are there so many meetings without doing anything?" Therefore we began to question, like Philipe Barreda and José; people with jobs and money, but who were with us. Therefore we began to say that we have to do something if we are Christian. Thus we had begun with reading Christian writings, since the cursillos were elitist, middle class or higher. But we began to work for all the poor, the workers, and the campesinos, without a middle class, except as leaders. Thus it grew into people working for Christ and we came to discover the documents of John XXIII and Vatican II, and we gained the trust of the pueblo. (Journal Entry 740, 21 October 1985)

Of course the dialectic nature of the meetings can be questioned. How much were the agents of change, the middle-class leadership, religious and lay, responsible for giving cursillo and CEB participants their interpretation of the social situation? When questioned on this Padre José responded:

Yes they are leaders, but their option is with the poor and to exclude none. It is certain that the CEBs were almost always born through religious or a priest of the middle class, but afterwards the same community questioned the priests. (Journal Entry 612, 8 October 1985)

Maria provided an example of this development of critical discernment concerning their religious leaders:

Padre Felix of El Rosario [her barrio and parish in Esteli] was with the revolution before, but now no. These [type of] priests want exploitation of the person by the person; to maintain their power. Our working, our concern is with the poor. . . . Padre Felix is a hypocrite, not sincere. We need a priest that is sincere, interested in educating each person, forming Christians and change. . . . We need to work with people who want to know, to give them *conciencia* [consciousness/conscience] of what it is to be a Christian, what it is to be in process. We can't do this without spiritual direction, but organized by a priest who has *conciencia*, not one with a big bank account. (Journal Entry 659, 21 September 1985)

Even though the CEBs and cursillos purport to be dialogic, the question of authority, in this instance the leadership function, appears to be critical if a dialogue is to be developed and maintained. We also would do well to remain critical of the role of the leadership. Facilitating dialogue but providing the documents to be studied and the mode of analysis may be leading participants to another interpretation of their social situation, but that is not necessarily open or consensual and may very well be submitting the members to merely another form of authority imposed, albeit more democratically, from the outside. This would be employing the guise of democracy by providing select authorities, such as Marxist analysis, as the sole means of analysis, and then engaging members in the interpretation of reality using only these limited, and so biased, tools.

Juan's testimony of how the cursillos and the CEBs were precursors for the Civil Defense Committees, the local militia which resisted the military dictatorship, illustrates how the CEBs were criticized precisely for indoctrination to a revolutionary perspective:

And thus we [leaders of the cursillos and CEBs] began another type of work, to conscientize the people, politically; to give them an account of the economic political and social situation in which they are living. When the *guardia* [Somoza's military, the National Guard] found out, they began persecuting us, saying we were using religion for political purposes, and saying that we weren't Christian. Therefore the guardia killed some of us, like Guillermo was persecuted. Therefore we asked, "How can we be defended from the guardia?" It occurred to me to form an organization to protect us. Thus was born the organization of the *comites de barrios* [neighborhood committees, precursors of the CDC]. It was not formed by the Frente, but from our necessity. Therefore we created the comites de barrios. That was an idea like that of the Frente's but which we did for our own reasons. It's clear that when we established the idea of this organization, it was very simple but functional, for our own work, which today is called the Sandinista Defense Committees. (Journal Entry 740, 21 October 1985)

Similarly, Padre Philipe illustrates the critical and obscure point where organization for reflection on participants' lives and action blends into mobilization for political confrontation:

Since the church was the only place where they could speak; for example, a person disappeared, we would try every form to find him or her, public demonstrations. . . . People seeking the Way can't coincide with the oppression that was going on. Therefore to protect their lives I arranged the CEBs in the diocese of Esteli. At the same time the Frente was concerned with the problem of fighting to change the situation of the country. [He leaned over and taking the pen, made an horizontal line with a midway perpendicular intersecting line. He pointed to one end of the line or spectrum, and said:] On the one side there is me and the group [CEB]. [Pointing to the other end of the spectrum:] On the other side are those that are fighting [the Frente]. Therefore the question came, "How can a Christian participate?" I didn't have the answer, they did. I didn't say, "Yes." Together they discovered the future of their children; what was happening with their brothers. Somoza accused six priests. I wasn't included. One North American was expelled, and the others, Nicaraguans, continued here with difficulty and were detained for some time. And this is how the practice of this sort begin. . . . Thus the first form was to organize by manzana and by blocks. [Again he leaned over and taking the pen drew a rectangle (a *manzana*) containing six blocks.] Thus the Civil Defense Committee [CDC] was born in Esteli. In each manzana, if someone was captured, they would handle it within the manzana and blocks. In this manner they would organize for defense. But they could meet in the church. Therefore people of different manzanas met in the church and established good relations. Afterwards this was for political and military organizing, but now [after the Triumph] we [the CEBs] don't need that part, but rather to motivate and support, and this is how the CDC was formed in Esteli. At first it was just a barrio; how to protect it. But a barrio was too big. The priest therefore organized. . . . In the Triumph I rarely helped out, giving a ride to guerrilleros, but not transporting guns. (Journal Entry 844, 28 October 1985)

Juan explained how the CEBs finally became involved in the insurrectional fight:

When the Frente observed our work, we had good relations, but they were in their own place. They began visiting. . . . We had the people and so they came to us. That was at the house where I used to live. . . . One day the organizing reached a national level, with the rich of Nicaragua . . . also against Somoza's control of everything. . . . In Esteli, they knew of our organization, our *comite de barrio*, and of the Frente also. . . . They both [the organization of the rich and the Frente] asked us to join, and therefore we decided to help with the national stop [general strike]. . . . [The guardia] began persecuting the poor, and so we began to strike, communicating with the Frente. Therefore the strike was more violent. . . . Up to this moment we had spoken with the Frente and with the rich, but not about insurrection. But with the strike began our first insurrection working with the Frente. At that time there were three hundred men in Esteli to fight, and also all the organization of the barrios to support them. Therefore we entered directly into insurrection. (Journal Entry 740, 21 October 1985)

The liberation ideology, social analysis, and organizational skills learned in the CEBs finally led some members to the conclusion that armed struggle and participation in the FSLN as the revolution's vanguard was necessary. The model's characteristics of openness of membership, means of social analysis, consensus in decision making, and realization of the need for coordination with other groups, if the revolution was to succeed in overthrowing Somoza, led to the crossover in membership of some CEB and FSLN members. Indeed this was the conclusion of some of the priests themselves who took up arms, such as Padre Gaspar Garcia Laviana, a martyr of the revolution (Randall 1983, 84).

In Margaret Randall's *Cristianos en la revolucion*, religious and students from the Jesuit-directed University of Central America in Managua provide accounts of their involvement in the first development of the CEBs as study circles in the community. They testify to the leadership roles of the religious, such as Padre Uriel Molina, whose parish was the first focal point for the community, and Padre Fernando Cardenal, who recruited students from the university. Under the direction of the religious, the students, sometimes living in the community, including secondary school students, were prepared to lead cultural circles, "study circles with groups from the community, workers and people from the neighborhood who would come daily to the parish" (Randall 1983, 140). Like Padre Ernesto Cardenal's CEB on Solentiname, the religious founders were motivated by Vatican II and Medellín. Ernesto Cardenal attributes the first rule of the CEBs, "that there would be no rules," to the guidance of fellow Trappist Thomas Merton (19–22).

The students and religious recognized that this "Christian movement" as it expanded out into the barrios was "a movement of the petty bourgeois," the middle class, but as they became involved in the barrios, with the people, in "the work of organization," they came to realize that "the Christian vision" was to be at "the service" of el pueblo (the people) (Randall 1981– 82, 229, 234, 236). Fernando offers the understanding of Christianity fostered in this, the roots of the CEBs in Nicaragua:

It is false to say to a person: "I love you," if he is in a situation of injustice and I do nothing to alleviate the causes of that injustice. (Randall 1983, 156)

Maria explained the change in her life from participating in a cursillo:

It was the first time that I saw the Bible from the point of view of the reality in which we live. We studied the book of Exodus, where God said: "I have seen the suffering of my people, and I will save them, liberate them." And so we could just think in the same way of the suffering of the people there, in the barrio, do you understand? We dialogued with the people, and when we listened to one, well it was a tremendous testimonial . . . how he lives, his problems, and his faith that something would be done. (Randall 1981–82, 237)

Joaquin testified that the library used to guide the study circles in their social analysis included the Bible, works of liberation theologians, the documents of Vatican II and Medellín, the work of Camillo Torres, a South American priest turned guerrillero who died in combat, and later Marxist works (Randall 1983, 122). Through participation in the study groups with the poor of the barrio, Manuel testifies, "We arrived at a conclusion that the system that we had was bad and that we had to change it" (35).

The intergration into the FSLN was done on an individual basis, illustrating the openness of membership, yet with the consensual support of the community for the individual's decision. Members of the Frente admired the work of the CEBs and while attending their meetings invited participants to attend an FSLN meeting. Joaquin testified:

We discussed among ourselves, and the conclusion that I reached in that discussion, I remember, I'll never forget it, is that, the militancy of the Frente is an individual option, it could not be a collective choice. But the choice that each has to make as an individual, is one in which the collective helped. (Randall 1981–82, 217–18)

A partial list of those interviewed in Randall's manuscript, those students and barrio residents who participated in this community, among the first CEBs in Managua, and their positions at the time testifies further to the role of CEBs in providing revolutionary leadership. It includes the following government positions, held when the Sandinistas were in power: Joaquin Cuadra, Vice-Minister of Defense and Major General of the Sandinista Armed Forces; Roberto Gutierrez, Vice-Minister of Agricultural Development and Agrarian Reform; Salvador Mayorga, also Vice-Minister of Agricultural Development and Agrarian Reform; Alvaro Baltodano, Director of Combat Preparation and Military Instruction; Luis Carrion, Member of the National Direction of the FSLN and Vice-Minister of the Interior; Padre Ernesto Cardenal, Minister of Culture; Padre Fernando Cardenal, Minister of Education; Padre Angel Barrajon, Director of Department of Human Resources of the Ministry of Agriculture; Jose David Chavarria Rocha, a soldier in the Sandinista military; and Sister Maria Hartman, who works in the Nicaragua Commission for the Promotion and Protection of Human Rights (Randall 1983, 105–7). The consensual nature of the CEBs did not infringe on the openness of members to choose individually whether or not to join the FSLN, though the community assisted with that decision.

The above exposition of the freedom of each member of a CEB to decide individually whether or not to support the guerrilleros or even join in the armed struggle him/herself, and the question of the coordination of efforts with an external authority, in this case between the Frente and the CEBs, brings us to the remaining requisite characteristic of our model.

COORDINATION

Coordinated action, the second characteristic in our model of democratic organization for social transformation, was carried on by the CEBs after the Triumph as well. In Esteli, INSFOP served as the CEB central coordinating body after the loss of the bishop's support. Each meeting of the CEBs, particularly of INSFOP, concluded with the discussion question: "What actions should we take as a group in response to the problems we have been discussing?" Each participant gave their suggestions which were then discussed and reported back to the group as a whole where they were discussed again until, by consensus, certain actions were agreed upon and tasks delegated voluntarily.

At a barrio-level CEB meeting, that could mean something quite simple. In the case of a woman who had been abused and deserted by her husband, a woman in the CEB who was closest to her volunteered to go and visit and ask what she needed and what the community could do to help. More demonstrative of the coordination were the town-wide INSFOP meetings. The founding members of the CEBs in Esteli established INSFOP as a central organizing headquarters, for the purpose of forming CEBs and coordinating their work regionally. Four middle-class couples, the aforementioned Barredas included, donated a house and hired a director, Mario, a Mexican theologian with whom they had become acquainted when he had earlier served on the bishop's pastoral council. From INSFOP work was coordinated for inviting new members, holding cursillos, and developing CEBs in other barrios and in the countryside, even where the local priest might not be sympathetic to their work.

Representatives from each CEB would attend a biweekly INSFOP meeting which in dialogic and consensual format would solicit the concerns of the various CEBs and what actions the group would plan to address these problems. In attendance at these INSFOP meetings were one or two leaders from each barrio CEB. The regional coordination was still able to prevent authoritarian domination from within the group because of the structure of the meetings.

One regular biweekly INSFOP meeting which I attended serves as an illustration. The thirty-five representatives attending broke into smaller groups to discuss the questions: "What have been the major concerns of our community over the last weeks? What actions do you suggest we take to answer these problems?" In the reporting back to the group at large, a consensual means of coordination was obvious in that everyone's opinion was reported. Through discussion, coordinated activities were planned. I found this all the more remarkable, in a meeting I attended, since this format was adhered to even though at the time the heaviest contra attacks since the Triumph had encircled Esteli. It appeared obvious to me what the major concern was, but true to our model of democratic organization, the setting did not override the democratic process.

Because of heavy contra attacks, the primary problem arrived at consensually was, "How to help in the defense of the town?" The solutions varied and different members volunteered to coordinate or participate in different responses which came up through the discussions. Some agreed to visit mothers of sons who were fighting or who had been killed in the recent fighting to console them and find out how they could help them with their needs. Others felt it was necessary to fight the fear that had come to the farming area surrounding the town due to contra attacks on cooperatives. To do this, they decided to work in the bean fields, despite the threat of contra ambush, since the crop needed to be harvested. Still others felt that a vigil at the cathedral against "North American aggression" and in solidarity with Nicaraguan Foreign Minister Padre Miguel D'Escoto's fast for peace was necessary. After deciding on which actions the group would take, the representatives returned to their barrios and in the following days tried to solicit participation in these plans.

An essential part of the process of the CEB and INSFOP meetings was the application and reinterpretation of the ideology or, in this case, their traditional Catholic faith. At the particular INSFOP meeting which I have been discussing, one of the actions the group decided to continue was a procession of the Way of the Cross through the town of Esteli on Friday evenings. This is a traditional Catholic practice commemorating the passion and death of Jesus and is usually celebrated only during the forty days prior to Easter. Reinterpreting this traditional symbol, paralleling Nicaragua's suffering with that of Christ's, the CEB communities of Esteli, coordinated through INSFOP, decided to pray the Way of the Cross every Friday night until the "North American aggression and contra attacks stop." Pausing at the fifteen stations in the procession, the participants not only recalled the agony and death of Jesus but related each station to the suffering of Nicaragua at the hands of the North American–backed contra attacks. Thus, their traditional faith was reinterpreted through the participants' experience to support them and give meaning to their struggles. Picking beans on cooperatives targeted for contra attacks, public fasting in opposition to U.S.–backed contra attacks, and interpreting these attacks in terms of Nicaraguans' traditional religious faith are examples of the CEBs coordinating to support the revolution; symbolically, in the case of the fasting and processions, and practically in picking beans and coffee, needed harvests for food and revenue which were threatened by contra activity.

Nor was the strategic frontier area of Esteli in north central Nicaragua the only region with such widespread coordination. The northwestern part of the country north of Leon is also strategic because it too borders with Honduras from which the contra activities were initiated. In this northwestern region the CEBs have similarly been coordinated in a network called *El Bloque* (the Block) under the leadership of a Dominican religious, Padre Carlos. El Bloque contains a 185 CEBs centered in the town of Somotillo (Journal Entry 705, 2 October 1985).

The coordination did not stop at the regional level. Annual national assemblies with representives from each region also meet and following similar formats, discuss the problems confronting them and plan concerted action. Meeting at an international level CEB leaders refer to *El Encuentro de Solidaridad con El Monsignor Romero* (Solidarity Meeting with Monsignor Romero). Beginning in 1980 after the assassination of Oscar Romero, Archbishop of El Salvador, CEB representatives from the Philippines, Latin America, Europe, and even a few from North America gave "testimonies of what is happening in [our] countries" with theological reflection and "the question of how we can work in solidarity" (Journal Entry 612, 8 October 1985).

All of this coordination is the more remarkable when you consider that it is done not only as secondary organizations that are free of hierarchical control, but often with the hierarchy directly opposed. It also illustrates the complexity of the situation. Bishop Casaldaliga, a member of the National Brazilian Bishop's Conference (NBBC), visited Nicaragua during my research period. He travelled around from diocese to diocese, visiting CEBs, celebrating religious services in churches where pastors were sympathetic to the CEBs and expressing episcopal support for their work and for Foreign Minister Padre Miguel D'Escoto's fast for peace. This occurred at the same time that the Nicaraguan Cardinal Obando y Bravo was travelling around the country, visiting its cathedrals, speaking against both the revolution and the CEBs. Obando protested the Brazilian bishop's interference in Nicaraguan affairs and Casadaliga was later chastised by the Vatican. The cathedral doors were closed to Bishop Casaldaliga and Miguel D'Escoto on their visit to Esteli. They celebrated the Way of the Cross before the closed doors and mass in the barrio church of Padre José.

The need for legitimation by a figure of the central authority is a limitation on the democratic functioning of the CEBs and on the change agent's freedom to implement the model of democratic organization for social transformation in a given community. It will be the focus of the following prescriptive model. This limitation was inherited from their history and the social context of a traditionally hierarchical Catholic Church. We turn our attention now to this and other contradictions and limitations to democratic organization for social transformation found in the CEBs.

5

Limits and Contradictions

Leadership and authority are issues which consistently limit democratic organization for social transformation. In the context of a revolution this raises the question of indoctrination.

Indoctrination, defined at its simplest means to imbue with a doctrine. To "imbue" means to permeate or to saturate, implying a process that can be much more subtle than the repetitious reciting of approved slogans . . . most of us are indoctrinated throughout our lives; often without knowing it. (Winn 1983, 37)

In a more subtle form, then, one must look for indoctrination in issues of authority and ideology, in the leadership style, and in the selection of materials to be studied. As in Ranger's work in *Peasant Consciousness and Guerrilla War in Zimbabwe* (1985), both sides, the established authorities and the revolutionaries, tried to use religious ideology in their favor. Prior to the revolutionary movement, religious ideology and authority figures were used to get believers to do what the government required of them. In such a circumstance, the religious agent was representing the concerns of the central authority and not of the community-based organization. In Ranger's study, during the process of revolution religious authority figures and ideology were again employed, this time to develop a national socialist character (1985, 200, 342). Ranger states that in his case study congregations had changed "from unquestioning, passive recipients of the word coming from authority into challenging, analytical thinkers who recognize that degree of authority which is in themselves." Our evidence, however, points to a much more complex reality, with variations depending on leadership style, purpose of the meeting, and the development of participants.

The primary evidence of indoctrination and the lack of democratic organization in the CEBs to be used in this prescriptive model of the CEBs is direction from an authority outside the group itself and a leadership style which was not committed to a dialogic and consensual format. In such a case the agency of change, the individual agent or the community itself, was not able to execute these first and fourth requisites of the theoretical model. If particular encyclicals and council readings or even Scripture readings are selected for study and discussion, then who selects those readings and how is the discussion guided? A particularly vivid example was provided by the coordinating body of the CEBs in Managua.

When meeting with a priest who was leader of the promoting team for CEBs in Managua, I observed a similar organization to that in Esteli. Paralleling INSFOP, CEB representatives from the various barrios would meet every week or two weeks to coordinate activities. There was also a team giving two- or three-day seminars, based on the cursillos, for new members. As in Esteli, if the pastor of a particular barrio was not sympathetic to the CEBs then members of nearby CEBs or religious involved in the CEBs would "pass through" that barrio, organizing a CEB there. The padre lamented the poor relations with the bishop in Managua and contrasted it with Esteli where the bishop had first cultivated and been sympathetic to the CEBs. However, this center for CEB promotion in Managua also had ongoing classes in the history of Nicaragua and of the Church in Nicaragua. Included in these courses was a lesson on Christianity and Marxism, a case we will use to illustrate the issue of ideology as indoctrination by another authority, rather than as liberation guided by an ideology which is developed by the participants themselves.

I interviewed Armando, a twenty-six year old, married, working-class male who participated in the Managuan CEB coordinating body as a representative of his barrio's CEB, in which he had first become involved in 1977. When I asked Armando where he first learned of Marxism he said that before the revolution he had been "fearful" of Marxism since he had heard that it was "opposed to Christianity." He continued:

I first learned about Marxism in a simple book, *Lo Fantasma* [The Image], why people feared Marxism. It was given to me by a youth pastor, a priest, when I participated in the CEB formation. He left Managua, because he was kicked out by the bishop. . . . Christianity needs an analysis of reality in all levels and Marxism helps this. (Journal Entry 1031, 18 November 1985)

Similarly, Ignacio, a CEB leader in Esteli who had first been a laborer in Managua, referred to the issue of authority, whether it be the bishop or priest or the new means of analysis fostered by the cursillos. Even though he is critical of the bishops and praises the priests' integration into the life of el pueblo, note the leadership role of the priests and preferential treatment of religious:

I went [to a cursillo]. It awoke in me a clarification of the content of my faith. It was not too profound. It was a traditional theology, but it planted in me the sociopolitical problem of the country and *el compromiso cristiano* [Christian obligation] in this situation: for justice in the face of these social problems. It was not radical or revolutionary, but rather a question of, "How can we change this dictatorship and oppression?" . . . But in a moment things changed. There is the influence of priests who arrived in Esteli, and who gave a theological answer with the backing of the Church. They were more integrated with the pueblo, participating. This made the bishop feel he was losing authority and influence among the people. These [new priests] all left, were taken out, except for Padre José and Miguel [the Belgian missionaries] who were interested and met with the comunidade eclesia de base, and some Jesuits as in Ocotal, and Julio from Spain. The time arrived when the bishop tried to get rid of all of them. . . . It is more a popular Church. . . . We have to persevere against the hierarchy. Bishops are representatives of Christians and therefore we can't cut ourselves off from them but right now they are not listening. (Journal Entry 620, 10 October 1985)

The very deference to religious leadership and their need for legitimation is a limitation of the CEB's functioning as an independent democratic organization. As in Ranger's study, referred to above, both sides sought these leaders, in whom authority resided by very nature of their position, as legitimation for maintenance of the prerevolutionary status quo or for participation in the revolutionary process.

The question also remains, Where do the tools of analysis come from, since they become the authority? Perhaps the greatest criticisms that can be levelled at the CEBs is that the analysis of the social situation does not come from the people themselves. But no group exists in isolation from the world system of ideologies. Employing a liberation theology or a Marxist ideology in anaylsis may be more obvious to the observer because it is new to the area. Yet, traditional Catholic ideology as the people's means of interpreting their reality was also at one time an influence from an outside authority.

Any guide in analysis is open to the criticism of at least providing another authority external to the group and at worse another form of indoctrination. Take, for example, Ignacio's analysis of the Nicaraguan hierarchy's opposition to the revolution, when at first they supported it. He uses the following Marxist terminology:

To be able to maintain themselves [the hierarchy] within the pueblo the Cardinal had a role, and to do it he got money from the owners of the means of production, the bourgeoisie, and they pressured the same regime. The dictator, every day, took out more, got his fingers in business, banks, industry, and so he came into conflict with the bourgeoisie. They fought to defend their interests and so after the revolution they saw that they didn't have the power and so they left the Frente, and the hierarchy defends the bourgeoisie since the Frente assaulted the banks, etc. . . . Therefore the hierarchy, Obando, supported the revolution. But as the revolutionary process evolved and laws gave the pueblo consciousness of their class and their power and destroyed the powerful, giving bread to all, each followed their role. The bourgeoisie pulled out to defend their interests, the pueblo went to defend their rights and in this contest the hierarchy took a position by identifying with whom? Who they had defended before. Therefore Obando never changed his ideas. (Journal Entry 620, 10 October 1985)

But the Marxist analysis, of the ownership of the means of production and a class structure of society, was not newly introduced by the CEBs. Pre-Triumph religion textbooks in the Catholic high school of Esteli have a marked pro-Marxist message, making parallels between Marxism and Christianity. At the school, Colegio San Francisco, I interviewed a Marist brother who was director of catechesis or religious instruction for the diocese of Esteli. Marist textbooks, published in Venezuela, among more traditional religious themes discuss Marxist analysis and the reconciliation of Marxism with Christianity. Guidebooks made at the colegio for discussion instruct the catechesis to "discuss the war of liberation in Nicaragua" and to guide the explanation with the story of Moses and God's liberation of his people from bondage in Egypt. Questions of application include, "How can we help to liberate us more?" (Journal Entry 605, 9 October 1985).

The question here is not whether or not the CEBs use Marxist analysis to understand the socioeconomic history of their country, but rather, is it the sole source of analysis and is it done uncritically? The description of Latin American society cultivated by Medellín, Puebla, the liberation theologians, and so too by the CEBs was scriptural and scientific. It has emphasized liberation as opposed to development, "in part because as they read and attempted to find meaning in sacred scripture for Latin America they believed that liberation was a much truer biblical term than development" (Cleary 1985, 92). In the application of social science this description of the Latin American reality "was done largely by using dependency and class analysis." Recurrent themes in this analysis included "the existence of social sin (structural or institutionalized injustice), the spiral of violence . . . and the injustices of world capitalism" (84).

I raise this question concerning the source of analysis so as to recognize the very real limitation on the first characteristic of our model: that authority comes from the collectivity itself. The fundamental structural constraint on this is that no collectivity, nor its ideology, exists in isolation; it is influenced if not informed and instructed by bodies outside of itself. This makes our case studies vulnerable to the criticism that rather than the truth or the reality of the situation being discerned by the interaction of all members, in actuality the cursillos, CEBs, and the mass popular-education campaigns to be discussed in following chapters, are another form of indoctrination from outside, albeit from change agents, missionaries who appear to be sympathetic to the cause of the indigenous community.

Take, for example, a guidebook for pastoral work in an indigenous community which explains, in his own words, the experience of a religious missionary, Smutko, amongst the Miskito Indians in northeastern Nicaragua. He tried to apply

scientific studies, such as the sociology of religion . . . and an anthropological and situational catechesis . . . which allows the penetration and manipulation of another culture, from one perspective, or to preach the gospel in a form they understand and which has the social effect of enabling them to organize more effectively and to establish their priorities. (Smutko 1975, 10)

Although this scientifically armed missionary's self-proclaimed intentions are to organize the community and train the natural leaders in the defense of their rights, thus improving their living conditions, we cannot claim that the impact of the external agent, or this missionary establishing a comunidade eclesia de base, is in any way neutral or has a neutral effect on the community. Obviously he comes from a particular perspective. Even though he claims to help "the ethnic group to become the author of its own destiny rather than being the victim of the development of others," and that "to empower agents of change is better than being the agent of change" (10–19), he is in actuality, by his very organizing activity, an agent of change. And the more that that change challenges the pre-existing central authority the more likely that conflict will result. And when the conflict arises between the central authority and the authority from within the group, the role of the formulator of the community-based organization, the agent of change, is critical. Does his allegiance as representative rest with the central authority or with the community? Or is he somehow able to mediate between the two and effect macro-level change in the Church structure?

How does this organizing of a community and the inspiration of a new ideology "of liberation" (11) measure up to a theoretical model of democratic organization for social transformation? On the characteristic of authority, the CEB leader, whether the missionary religious or the local Delegate of the Word trained by the religious, is the change agent whose opinion most likely will be respected above that of other members of the group. Smutko in his work with the Miskito Indians realized this group dynamic. His first guideline for the establishing of a CEB reads: "To help the indigenous leaders form a structure for integral liberation (integral development) of their ethnic group and to defend their rights." The second tries to lessen the role of the missionary but nonetheless recognizes the danger inherent in their authority: "It is better that the organization and its goods are in the possession and control of the indigenous and that the missionary be only a facilitator" (11).

Two issues are involved here: Domination by an authority outside of the group and by an authority within the group. One, the question of who is the authority and where does the authority come from, concerns the first characteristic of our model and the community itself as the agency of change. Two, the natural differentiation that takes place in a group due to talents of the various members (Duberman 1972, 37) often results in particular individuals, founders and leaders, dominating the community as the agents of change. This deals with the fourth characteristic of consensus. I have referred to consensus as the structural means for achieving the ideal that authority is vested in the collectivity itself. Rothschild and Whitt, however, argue that all organizations are internally differentiated according to the individual differences and assets of each member (1986, 70).

By natural differentiation we mean that within the membership certain participants, who are, for example, eloquent in speech, are likely to be selected as the spokespersons representing the group. Another might be more knowledgeable of biblical or Marxist literature and so is given deference when social issues are analyzed using these sources. Another might be a popular socializer in the community who is thus given the task of organizing, passing door to door soliciting new members.

As in the directives for establishing CEBs and Smutko's experience among the Miskito, Delegates of the Word are chosen because they are "natural" leaders, those already respected as leaders in the community. Kincaid's study of a CEB's revolutionary role in El Salvador also comments on how organizational meetings are led by individuals identified and selected because of their leadership abilities (1987, 483). Jean-Jacques Rousseau claimed that participatory democracy would work in small groups where everyone knew each person present, and this has been supported by recent empirical research (Rothschild and Whitt 1986, 91–95). However, my observations of CEB meetings indicated that, even in these small familiar groupings, there were cases where the same leaders always directed the meetings. In other more rare and more democratic instances, leadership was rotated, sometimes by voting. Even in this case of rotation by election, the pool of those selected as leaders, and who would accept the nomination, was relatively small in relation to the organization as a whole.

Furthermore, the leaders' authority often rested in their position, such as that of the religious or the Delegate of the Word, their role as representatives of the central authority, the Church hierarchy, and in their familiarity with a document, such as the Bible, which carried great weight with the group. There appeared to be a greater consensuality at meetings where members were equally familiar with the proceedings and where there was greater structure to facilitate the input of each member.

The INSFOP meeting in Esteli which I have referred to was clearly run by the religious, Padres José and Miguel. They stood at the front of the room, introduced the meeting, and solicited responses from the smaller groups which had broken down to discuss and report on the guide questions, "What have been the major problems confronting us these past weeks?" "What is our response?" (Journal Entry 261, 24 August 1985). Since there are leaders in such organizations, the degree to which they are consensual then depends on the extent to which the leader willingly shares authority with members—which depends on the egalitarian ideology—as well as on personal characteristics of the leader, the familiarity of members with the proceedings, and the extent to which the structure of the organization solicits equally the input of all members. This extent to which the organization is consensual will determine the extent to which the community itself is the agency of change, not dependent on the directives of a particular leader or change agent.

In the case of the INSFOP meeting there appeared to be a great degree of consensus because the structure solicited the input of each member on the questions and then reported these back to the larger group where Padre Miguel put them on a board for further discussion. However, there were individual meetings of CEBs which appeared to be dominated by the leader, in one case the Delegate of the Word. In one such observed occasion the leader called a typical meeting for reflection on a passage of Scripture and application of that passage to the participants' lives. At the meeting the leader not only selected and read the passage but on reviewing the transcript of the meeting, was the person speaking more than 50 percent of the time! (Journal Entry 392, 5 September 1985) This is hardly dialogic or consensual.

This could be somewhat due to the participants' lack of familiarity with the exercise and having to be drawn out by the leader. However, in this case most participants had attended and participated in prior such meetings. More likely in this instance it was because of the leader's style. After each person commented on the reading the delegado was all too willing to jump in and comment on their comment, referring to the scriptural passage another time. His greater familiarity or expertise with the document and with discussion and offering his opinion was obvious, but it did little for making the meeting more dialogic or consensual. If anything it did not provide silences during which others in attendance might be drawn into participation. This anomaly indicates the limits placed on our model by the individual leader's style and the necessity of adhering to the structural and ideological characteristics of openness and consensus.

Although the latter Bible study group had a dozen participants, a third of the number of the INSFOP meeting—and assuming they were more familiar with each other than at the INSFOP meeting because they were all neighbors from the same barrio—it was actually less participatory because of the style of the facilitator or leader, the absence of structure for soliciting and giving equal weight to each participant's input, and less familiarity and apparent ease of participants with the format of the meeting. The CEB leader's specialized knowledge of the document also limited others' participation.

Furthermore, the extent to which a leader adheres to a dialogic and consensual format will depend not only on the structure of the meeting, but also on his/her adherence to the ideological concomitant that each person's opinion is equal and necessary for the group's self-direction.

One other observed CEB meeting should further illustrate the problem of consensus and its relationship to the issue of authority. At a barrio's CEB communal meal service or agape, a Delegate of the Word could be clearly seen to be directing the service. An upper-middle-class member who had been one of the four establishing couples of INSFOP, he had provided the corn that had been used to make the meal. Selecting particular participants from the meeting to read from the national CEB newspaper, *El Tayacan*, the religious service was highly structured. Both the Scripture readings and the reflections on them in revolutionary Nicaragua were provided in the newspaper. These readings were interspersed with songs, CEB hymns, which another Beligian religious, a sister, chose in discussion with some of the women. The service was concluded with a distribution of the cornmeal, eating and singing, and seemed to be enjoyed by all participants. Before the final hymn a letter from the Frente Sandinista was read, calling on all Estelianos to hold firm in face of the contra attacks which were taking place at the time, the worst since the Triumph (Journal Entry 39, 4 August 1985).

Although clearly more of a religious service than a meeting, I have included this for comparison with the other two CEB meetings because of the apparent lack of a dialogic. It demonstrates that meetings can also be overstructured to the detriment of democratic participation. In this case, providing people with readings and commentary is counterproductive to dialogue and consensus and can be doctrinaire. The structure must build in dialogue. If a group is going to replace one external authority for another, or if an individual leader from within the group becomes a directive change agent rather than consensually making the community the agency of change, then it is not a democratic organization in that it lacks independence from central authority and the right to self-determination where authority resides in the collectivity. Of course, this does not preclude the use of whatever documents the group chooses to reflect on. The group has the right to be informed by whatever sources are available. However, it does bring to question who selects the documents for study and who provides the interpretation?

In the case of the last CEB service reviewed, the documents and commentary were both selected and provided by an outside authority, *El Tayacan*, albeit a publication of a pro-CEB, prorevolutionary religious group in Managua. The inclusion of the letter from the Frente in the service was also an act of an external authority. The comment of my Managua subject family's father, a prorevolutionary, anti-Sandinista, traditional Catholic who did not participate in the CEBs is understandable. In asking him why he did not chose to participate in the CEBs, he responded, "The CEBs are merely tools of the Sandinistas" (Journal Entry 1101, 14 December 1985).

One might be tempted to argue that the setting of a contra attack (defense helicopters could be heard bombing) overrode the democratic process in the CEB service. However the same contra attack existed at the time of the observed INSFOP meeting. The INSFOP meeting, on the other hand, was also structured, but structured in such a way that invited all participants to contribute without attempting to predispose them. I found it quite remarkable, as an observer, that at a time when the town was ringed about by contras that the discussion should still be guided by the same weekly questions: "What are the greatest concerns confronting us and what is our response?" This is an indication, however, that the setting, in this case the emergency of contra attack, need not necessarily override the democratic process, if the meeting is structured to guarantee egalitarian dialogue. Both the INSFOP and CEB agape were held at the time of the contra attacks, yet the INSFOP meeting maintained the democratic process because it was structured to do so, soliciting from each participant their concerns. The CEB service, on the other hand, was not structured to include dialogue or consensus. It provided readings, commentary, or even interpretation. There was neither space for dialogue nor a soliciting of participants' concerns or understanding of the readings.

It is important to ask who provides the materials studied and what is their intention. Are they to facilitate the group's self-determination or to provide an alternative external authority and interpretation of the "reality" of the situation? In the case of the INSFOP meetings the questions were general enough that they could be applied to all circumstances and yet solicit the response of participants. But can the same be said of a Marxist analysis of the socioeconomic situation: Who are the owners of the means of production and who works for whom? Is this not to lead the group to another interpretation of their reality provided by another external authority? And yet, if the organization is to fulfill the requisite of openness, members should be entitled to use the tools of this analysis as well as those of dialogue or traditional scriptural interpretation for discerning their reality and planning their actions.

Whether or not the tools of analysis are used to indoctrinate or liberate is answered in the extent to which the group is enabled to participate democratically in the transformation of their society; the extent to which the group is free to use whatever documents and analysis they wish, dialogically and consensually, in the interpretation of their reality. Of course in order to use those tools they need to be taught so that the knowledge is not an elitist asset which is only used by the intellectual. This brings up yet again the question of authority—does it reside in the leader as change agent, or in the community itself as the agency of change? Who selects the tools of analysis? If they are sociological are they functionalist or Marxist, if they are theological are they traditional or liberation?

The question of authority is related to the concept of CEBs as secondary organizations, that is, independent of an external established authority. As a democratic organization the issue of authority also has an internal dimension, that is, who is the authority within the group, from whence is the authority derived—either a person such as an establishing missionary, or a lay leader, the Delegate of the Word, or from written material such as the Bible, documents of reforming Church councils, papal social encyclicals, or Marxist historical analysis that were referred to by CEB members? And are these not external and is their interpretation or application arrived at in a democratic consensual manner or by the authority of a leader's position? Despite the complexity of the Nicaraguan situation and the variations in CEBs, several conclusions can be drawn concerning the functioning of democratic organizations for social transformation before turning to other cases for further verification and qualifications.

6

Initial Conclusions

We have constructed a theoretical model or ideal type of a democratic organization for social transformation based on theories of democratic organization, conflict, and revolution. This model's four requisite characteristics indicate what one should find in an organization if it is democratic and transformatory, that is, engaged in empowering previously disenfranchised persons. The CEBs purport to be such an organization. It becomes clear after reviewing their history and functioning and measuring them by our model's requisites that the CEBs are not the ideal democratic organization for social transformation. Despite the CEBs' limits, however, this research has demonstrated the contradictory nature of democratic organization in real-life situations, has provided a theoretical model for the measuring of such organizations, and has illustrated how some of the requisites for such an organization were carried out in a descriptive model of the CEBs. We also now have indications of what circumstances are favorable to such an organization, and under what conditions the organization is likely to fall short of its democratic and revolutionary goal. Using the four requisite characteristics of our model, we will next review these findings in a prescriptive model of what would be required of the CEBs if they are to measure up to our ideal type model.

AUTHORITY

The overriding limitation on democratic organization for social transformation is the social context in which the organization finds itself. Though the CEBs attempted to function independently, this was limited by their placement within a traditionally hierarchical Church structure. The CEBs were dependent on external agents, missionaries or bishop, for their initial cultivation. Even once established a coordinating body was necessary for their continued success, which was undoubtedly inhibited by the hierarchy and a traditional ideology which regarded hierarchical endorsement as necessary. When that support was not provided by the domestic bishop, a foreign bishop was imported and paraded around for legitimation. The ideology of the CEBs is not so developed democratically as the ideal type requires. Actual instances fall short in the belief in self-determination and that authority resides in the collectivity.

The Sandinista encouragement of the CEBs and use of them as means of promoting their interests also raises the question of independence from a central authority, even if that authority is supportive. It appears that the democratic organization is most likely to succeed in its goal of social transformation when protected by a central or external authority which heeds the organizations' suggestions. And yet being independent from and at the same time requiring a central authority's support is a difficult enterprise to maintain.

There is always a context. No community exists in isolation. This is well illustrated by the selection of materials for tools of analysis. Whether they be Marxist economic analysis, liberation theological analysis, or a traditional scholastic theology which promotes compliance, each was imported to the indigenous community at some time. It appears that the best guard against indoctrination and manipulation is the third characteristic of the model, openness. Being open to all sources and analyses a community can select the interpretation, or combination of approaches, which they feel best applies to their situation. The case of the CEBs, however, demonstrates that the reality of the situation rarely allows such well-informed decision making or a complete openness of membership. Those who formed the CEBs and later their leaders selected the analyses they favored and shared these skills with participants. This raises the issue of internal authority and consensus.

COORDINATION

There will always be the macro-level context to which the local democratic organization must relate. Yet, the necessity to coordinate the efforts of the revolutionary organizations if the revolution is to succeed is an inherent contradiction with independence from a central authority. Coordination also limits democratic participation because it requires representation, a mediator. The mediator can become too readily the agent of change, as either mouthpiece for the central authority or director of the community. True democratic organization for social transformation requires the community itself to be the agency of change, and the representative to be its mouthpiece. This contradiction produces a tension which, I would argue, in the last instance is necessary if social transformation is to succeed; particularly because coordination is necessary in the face of external threats. Coordination also requires the selection of representatives which in turn encourages elite membership and specialists, both inhibiting consensus. Coordination is most likely to maintain the democratic organization's goals if its representatives truly represent the interests of its constituents and if representative and organization are more concerned with coordinating those interests with the central authority than with promulgating the central authority's self-conceived agendas.

OPENNESS

Because the democratic organization functions best when small, the groups so organized are often composed of those who share similar interests. Yet this characteristic requires an openness of membership. Inherently, however, not everyone will want to join. Thus the CEBs are a highly motivated core of the parish. Yet for this core not to become an elitist revolution, its members, the vanguard, must adhere to an ideology which recognizes the self-worth and rights of all members of the community, including those who are not participants. For persons who were previously marginalized and disenfranchised this requires an ideology and exercises which develop their self-esteem as liberation theology and the cursillos did. Membership in alternative organizations is also a possibility for empowering those who choose not to join a CEB. This is the case with some CDC members and members of other mass organizations which we will study, such as the farmer's association. There are always those, however, if not the majority, who choose not to participate as members in any of the revolutionary organizations.

CONSENSUS

Perhaps the most difficult characteristic of the democratic organization for social transformation to maintain is that of consensus. Besides the more obvious of the religious or Delegates of the Word being the leaders and agent of change, communities have "natural leaders," individuals who are more talented in leadership. And whom are these agents responsible to? Are they accountable to the Church hierarchy, superiors of their religious orders, or are they accountable to the CEB and its members? The natural differentiation according to talents also runs the risk of investing unequal authority in the leader as a specialist who knows what is best and can make the decisions. This makes the leader, rather than the community, the change agent. This does not transform the power base in the manner in which we have been speaking of empowering. Deference is often paid to the leader's opinion, contradicting the egalitarian value of each member's contribution.

Since this seemed inevitable in the CEBs, the democratic organization appears to succeed to the extent to which the leader adheres to structure and ideology which guarantee dialogue, practices self-restraint, and promulgates belief in the value of each person and their opinion. Again this consensual format requires training of participants in skills of dialogue. To avoid domination by the internal authority or leader, participants must also become skilled in the functioning of the organization. In the case of the CEBs this would require training in the application of theology to their daily lives and in social analysis. Often that would be as simple as encouraging participants to give their opinions and interpretations of their realities; convincing them that they are the experts in their own lives.

Yet because the adherence to a dialogic and consensual format often depends on the leader's style and commitment, and the level of involvement and familiarity with procedure of other members, it is open to abuse. As in the case of some CEB meetings, even the best intentioned leader can ignore democracy within the organization in haste to achieve what he/she considers the best interests of participants. Listening is a vital requisite for leaders. Adhering to a structure and ideology of dialogue and consensus, despite the setting, is a necessity if the democratic organization is to transform by empowering participants.

Having reviewed what our model and Nicaraguan case have taught us of democratic organization for social transformation, we next proceed with the comparative part of our study. Following Glaser and Strauss (1967) and Stinchcombe's (1978) advice, referenced in our introduction, this will be to further qualify the model. We will study data on the development and functioning of the CEBs in El Salvador, Guatemala, and Brazil. What do the differing national contexts and internal dynamics suggest concerning the viability of democratic organization for social transformation?

Our analysis will be guided by the four characteristics of the model, with particular emphasis on what appears to be the crucial characteristics in the performance of the CEBs in differing contexts: the relationship to a central authority. How do the CEBs function in relation to the government or Church hierarchy? How do they fare where they lack the support of any central authority, or where they are supported by the hierarchy?

In order to further revise our theoretical model in studying its applicability, I will expand the case studies to include other organizations engaged in social transformation that purport to be democratic. I begin with a comparative analysis of the CEBs in differing national contexts.

7

A Comparative Analysis of Christian Base Communities

The CEBs throughout Latin America share a common history already reviewed: growth out of the experience of Latin American poverty and political oppression, the application of historical exegesis in the development of a native ideology—liberation theology—and the application of social science in social analysis (Houtart 1964) and to community organization as a means of empowering the previously marginalized and disenfranchised in their self-direction. The resulting empowerment through organizational attempts to improve their participants' lot inevitably brought the CEBs into opposition and then conflict with the traditional authorities unaccustomed to having their power challenged in such a democratic popular fashion. In Nicaragua this opposition came from the pre-Triumph government, the Anastasio Somoza dictatorship, and the post-Triumph Church hierarchy.

We will see this pattern repeated in various forms in each of the three countries to be studied now. The success, failure, or even the continued existence of the CEBs will illustrate the importance of the first characteristic of our model: the relationship of the democratic organization to the central authority, be that state or Church. Religious missionary orders, or progressive bishops, acting as change agents, set about establishing CEBs. Yet with time, conflict—in some cases even with the establishing authority—came to characterize the CEBs' relationships with central authorities external to the CEBs themselves.

The extent to which the CEBs in each case were able to continue in the face of opposition is an indication of their independence and commitment to an ideology of self-determination, as well as the overriding importance of the national political context. In order to at first thrive, and then survive in the face of opposition, the CEBs required a coordination with each other and with other parties that promoted the same interests of social transformation. That coordination was provided in Nicaragua by the missionary religious and expanded to interface with the revolutionary vanguard, the FSLN, through individual crossover in membership, or by coordination with other revolutionary mass organizations, such as the Civil Defense Committees.

In the following comparisons, we will review the history of the CEBs in each country, their context, and in more detail how they functioned in particular case CEBs. The comparative analysis will be based on the four requisite characteristics of our model. In this way we will be able to examine further the emergent patterns of what inhibits or enables a CEB to thrive as a democratic organization engaged in social transformation.

EL SALVADOR

The El Salvadoran CEBs, like those in Nicaragua, were dependent for their establishment on the external influence of reform-minded religious. In El Salvador that came from the direction of Archbishop Chavez, employing predominantly native religious, whereas in Nicaragua the CEBs were established in a unsystematic manner by various missionary religious (Montgomery 1982, 212–13). (The CEBs in the dioceses of Esteli and Bluefields were exceptions where the bishop was directly involved in their cultivation.)

In our Nicaraguan case study, Padre José testified that he and Padre Miguel and Sister Graciela, Belgian missionaries working with the CEBs in Esteli, had to leave El Salvador because of the threats to their lives from government forces alarmed at their organizing activity. Here, as in all of our cases, the religious' experience of the oppressive poverty of their parishioners was interpreted by the renovations suggested in Vatican II and Medellín (Prendes 1983, 268). These renovations included the application of social sciences to "institutionalized violence" and the "structural sin" of poverty.

Kincaid, in his research of the revolutionary activities of one town in El Salvador, places the responsibility for the success of the peasant uprising in Aguilares squarely on the organizing efforts of the CEB. Other sources likewise attribute the rapid growth of El Salvador's popular organizations and the training of hundreds of revolutionary leaders in organizational skills to the CEBs' role in "organizing and *concienticizing* the people" (Montgomery 1982, 220).

The Jesuits took the parish of Aguilares under their direction and together with other religious orders in other parishes of San Salvador set up "training centers for lay leaders from different areas of the country" (Prendes 1983, 275). Kincaid's study of Aguilares found that, once formed the CEBs "began to address problems of land tenure, employment and social justice—pitting peasants against estate owners and local security forces," and drawing the community, now organized around its problems, inextricably into rebellion (Kincaid 1987, 484).

In a familiar pattern, Kincaid describes how religious, organizing the CEBs, built on traditional community bonds, selecting CEB representatives for their leadership abilities. The work of the CEBs was particularly important in the face of what Kincaid terms "a strong trend toward declining village autonomy" and cohesiveness due to the penetration of national structures. These structures were not just political, military, and economic market forces, but include the founding of the CEBs themselves, although the penetration of national religious structures was designed to counter village disintegration by helping to organize the community (Kincaid 1987, 483–90). Characteristic of all of our CEB cases, their foundation was dependent on a traditional religious authority—religious orders of priests and sisters—which was also responsible for the coordination with other CEBs. In time this dependence on the central religious authority for legitimation in a hierarchically structured Church would limit the CEBs' ability to function independently.

From Kincaid's and various other accounts of those involved with different CEBs, we are able to reconstruct their functioning in El Salvador. A testimony given by Padre David Rodriguez speaks of his organizing work with CEBs in his parish of Tecoluca in El Salvador and the resulting conflict with the hierarchy and government. Padre Rodriguez describes his efforts "to overcome the alienatation of those who only hear," in the CEB's Bible study groups:

We discovered that the campesino grows more when he speaks his own words than when he only listens. An individual who finds a place to speak his word and to be heard awakens . . . takes consciousness of his dignity . . . and begins to give his support in the construction of his own destiny. (1976, 34).

The reference to self-esteem and dialogue skills essential to the model's third and fourth characteristics—openness and consensus—are apparent.

As in Nicaragua, he gives account of how "little by little" from the Bible reflection groups arose individuals who came to form the CEB. Padre Rodriguez describes the radicalization of the CEB to participation in land seizures. His account moves from a Bible reflection discussion of "When we say 'Give us this day our daily bread,' what are we asking for?" to the group's responses of "The bread for tortillas, the bread of wisdom, the bread of the Eucharist, the bread of the word of God," to "We struggle so that every brother has the bread needed for living . . . so that all will be fed." The actual movement of the CEB to land seizures he describes merely in oblique terms: "Little by little they were consolidated and we learned and discovered the fallacy of the system in which we live, that has made our faith, 'an opiate of the pueblo' " (35–37).

It seems apparent that the ideology of "opiate of the masses" came from outside the community, though the community applied that to its own situation. Yet the liberation theology, the dialogue over what daily bread means for the participants in their existential situation, is characteristic of the third and fourth requisites of our model. By giving value to the opinion and words of the campesino, openness and consensus are cultivated. Evidenced in this report of Padre Rodriguez are the ideological concomitance of the self-worth of each individual and the egalitarian belief in self-direction by the full participation of the members, both which characterize the requisites of our model of democratic organization for social transformation.

One might hastily conclude that this is evidence of ideological and structural manipulation from an outside force rather than empowerment of a community. However, as Nicaraguan post-Triumph Church histories are quick to point out, the traditional scholastic theology and parochial structure were also imposed from outside by missionaries, with less opportunity for dialogic participation by the indigenous community.

Padre Rodriguez goes on to describe the questions that were asked to guide discussion:

To understand false and true humility we only ask these questions: The young who are studying, why are they studying? To serve themselves or to serve others, above all those who are most needy? If they have their degree who do they serve with their degree; the powerful to become more powerful or the weak to help them discover their dignity? (36)

Though the earlier mentioned "opiate of the pueblo" is clearly a Marxist allusion, the above reference and the following are less so, but rather indicate the greater importance of a religious ideology of liberation. "The principle points of Bible reflection" reveal the influence of liberation theology:

1. God wants all to be well;

2. Humans went against the will of God;

3. God the Father asked his Son to reconstruct his plan;

4. Christ wants his plan realized not by angels but by men of good will;

5. Christ will triumph: wisdom over ignorance, justice over injustice, liberty over slavery. (38)

In either case, Marxism or liberation theology, the ideology is not so much manipulative as it provides another means of analysis of the participants' social reality. Neither analysis inspired by Marxist ideology—"the opiate of the pueblo"—nor liberation theology—"Christ wants his plan realized not by angels but by men"—is manipulative precisely because they are referenced in a dialogic format—"what are we asking for . . . who do they serve?" In asking, "What does this mean to you, in your everyday situation?" the particular ideology is merely used as a means of analysis, at the service of the community. In this way the change agent provides his knowledge and skills of social analysis at the service of the community, empowering it, making the community itself the agency of change.

Padre Rodriguez describes the resulting practices of the community which grew out of the CEB organization and reflection groups, and the conflict with the authorities which ensued. First there was the formation of savings and loans cooperatives in January 1971. Second, in 1972, when the leader of the government's political party came to town to organize its party for the election, the community response was a great abstention from voting. Voting rose in 1974 and 1976. The third conflict, Padre Rodriguez describes as the taking of land prior to the 1974 land reform, and then afterwards because the cost of the land was too high. The result was that the Salvadoran National Guard came and seized the land, killing and raping. On May 7, 1975, a fellow priest was captured and "martyred." The fourth conflict occurred when the community took more land. Such organizing led the CEB into conflict not only with the secular authorities but with the church hierarchy as well (41–50).

The interface between CEB and revolutionary activity is even more clearly illustrated in the case of Suchitoto, one of the strongest bases of the *Faribundo Martí Liberacion Nacional* (FMLN). It illustrates that openness to coordination with other mass organizations and revolutionary groups developed from the community's need to coordinate action if they were to achieve social change. Beginning work in 1968, within a few months Padre Jose Inocencio Alas had cultivated thirty-two CEBs in the parish. Montgomery describes how clandestine political action by young revolutionaries grew apace with the conscientizing work of the CEBs. Five years later, in 1974, representatives of campesinos, student and teacher organizations, and labor unions, gathered in the Basilica of the Sacred Heart in San Salvador to form the first of the mass popular organizations, the United Popular Action Front. Padre Alas and members of the National Resistance, the political faction of the People's Revolutionary Army, agree that the creation of the United Popular Action Front (the National Resistance's mass political organization) is a "clear case" of "a popular, revolutionary organization which grew directly out of the" organizational work of the CEBs (1982, 213–14).

In yet another case, Pablo Galdamez, a missionary priest, describes the organization of a CEB and its progress over a ten-year period. Its creation in a new urban slum on the outskirts of San Salvador is characteristic. From its inception it confronted the problem of lack of cohesiveness in such settings: building community was the essential groundwork for organization.

The community meetings bound us closer and closer together. The doors were open. We said hello to one another, we went to one another's houses. . . . We learned to search out the solution to our problems together . . . we felt strong. This was because we were united. (1986, 30)

The analysis of their problems started very simply:

Carlitos taught us that sickness wasn't the result of irresponsibility. Sickness came from unsanitary conditions. And unsanitary conditions were the result of poverty. We also discovered that children's sicknesses were almost always due to malnutrition. And we learned that children weren't malnourished because their mothers were irresponsible. They were malnourished because their mothers were poor. (22).

This CEB's organizing activities progressed from obtaining electricity, to water, to a co-op land tract for housing (30–31). A sample of the CEBs' social analysis is provided in this CEB's confronting the problem of unemployment:

The structures of sin [are] terribly strongly rooted in capitalist society. . . . Schools only open their doors to those who can pay the tuition. Our best land is used to raise crops for export—crops that bring in foreign capital, while our people go hungry and we have to import beans and rice. (47–48)

The ideology of self-worth and the realization of the necessity of coordination is expressed in this hymn from the Mass of the CEBs:

When the poor believe in the poor,
That's when we'll be free to sing . . .
When the poor seek out the poor,
And we're all for organization,
Then will come our liberation. (36)

While the CEBs continued to develop their own ideology (Galdamez 1986, 51), "the bourgeoisie joined the Government" in accusing them of "Communist indoctrination" (Prendes 1983, 278) and subversion (Galdamez 1986, 88).

There are several common elements in these cases which we have just reviewed. As in Nicaragua and the other cases to be studied, CEBs were developed in response to worsening conditions for the poorest and most marginalized, usually associated with the loss of land. At the time in El Salvador, .07 percent of the landowners held 40 percent of the land, while 40 percent of all rural families were landless (Burke 1976, 476–79). In each nation studied, the impetus for the organized action of the CEBs was the Church's previous neglect of the most marginalized and poorest in outlying rural areas or urban slums, the work of reform-minded clergy inspired by Vatican II and Medellín, and some form of political and economic oppression. In each case rural land was lost by traditional untitled campesinos to expanding agribusinesses, or in the case of Suchitoto to a government-sponsored hydroelectric dam. Or displaced campesinos moving to the edge of expanding urban centers were unable to find adequate housing or employment. This context taken into consideration, religious leadership was of primary importance in developing the CEBs—which brings up the question of agency with regards to the relationship to authority.

As stated in the model, the democratic organization is to be free of the control of the central and external authority with authority residing in the collectivity itself. But the context of the CEBs in no case permitted this because of the traditional hierarchical structure of the Church, the ideological deference to the religious leadership, be that bishop or priest, and the interference of the state with which the CEBs inevitably came into conflict. That the CEBs challenged the hierarchy at all is a testimony to the effectiveness of the new ideology of liberation theology and the leadership style of local religious who adhered to a dialogic and consensual structure. After all, the CEBs were themselves established by religious—priests or missionaries. The relatioinship of the El Salvadoran CEBs to the Church hierarchy further illustrates the contradictory nature and resulting tension of the relationship of the democratic organization to the central authority.

As in Nicaragua, religious leadership was instrumental in the establishment of CEBs in El Salvador. As with the CEPA in Nicaragua, the CEBs in El Salvador often started out around cooperativist projects and training centers for lay leaders, Delegates of the Word; both founded by religious (Prendes 1983, 270). Once trained, lay leaders were subject to repression because, as Bishop Rivera y Damas, a supporter of the CEBs, stated:

They were noticeable not only because of their complete, conscious and active participation in the Liturgical celebrations . . . but also for their actions in favour of Justice: strengthening peasant organizations, helping in the diffusion and study of pertinent Labour Laws, struggling for basic services and for just wages, and for dignified re-location. (Prendes 1983, 275)

The revitalization of the Church in El Salvador, especially in education and becoming active in rural areas, was largely due to the incorporation of the laity into Church activities. Though led by religious—sisters, brothers, and priests—this incorporation met with resistance from the hierarchy, notwithstanding the support of some bishops. Concerning our model's second characteristic of coordination, even here the CEBs were at first dependent on the central authority, the existing Church structure. It was largely due to the efforts of "progressive priests and laymen" that the Church journal and radio became a means of coordination, "diffusion and normalization," of the CEB experiences throughout the country (269–70).

When the empowered CEBs "evolved towards the renovation of the ecclesiastical structure itself," as in the First Week of the National United

Pastoral, in 1970, most of the hierarchy absented themselves from the encounter, intending "to distort the conclusions arrived at" in this "inauguration of a 'new Church model' " (268–69). Archbishop Oscar Romero provides an illustration of the tension of this issue of authority in the El Salvadoran CEBs.

Before becoming archbishop of San Salvador, Romero was critical of the CEBs and supported the violent closing of the national university in 1972, stating "to the effect that it was a good idea to close down such a hotbed of Communist activities." When criticized for this support by the CEBs, Romero accused them of "disobedience to ecclesiastical authorities and of mixing politics with the Eucharist" (Galdamez 1986, 54–55). Upon becoming archbishop, Romero was "converted" (55) and became the greatest supporter of the CEBs and popular organizations, creating a political unity of the various organizations (Prendes 1983, 289–93). This indicates a limitation and contradiction of the model: in an ideal type the democratic organization is free of the central authority. The support of the central authority, in this case members of the Church hierarchy, facilitated and strengthened the CEBs in their coordination with other popular organizations and in the face of repression by another central authority, the state.

Though the CEBs developed from the leadership of religious, they came into conflict with the hierarchy's conservative elements. Their criticisms of the hierarchy and opposition to the repressive state oligarchy illustrates the difficulty in their independent functioning as secondary organizations. Yet the need for the leadership of religious brings to question their ability to act independently even once established. Can democratic organization for social transformation spring spontaneously and indigenously from within such traditionally authoritarian structures? For their continued success, every indication from our case studies illustrates that this leadership is still needed. Our research also indicates that for the CEBs to continue in the face of the hierarchy's opposition, the agents of change, the establishing religious, must themselves side with the communities against the hierarchy—must choose whose interests they serve. This was the case in March 1978, when 300 priests, nuns, and monks throughout the country made public an address accusing the papal nuncio of siding with the government repression. In reaction conservative bishops censured their priests involved and in some cases even suspended them (Alas 1982, 190–93).

In the Nicaraguan case, we heard Maria, a CEB member, criticize a previously pro-CEB priest who had turned against the CEBs. This is an illustration of CEB independence. But even here the continued functioning of the CEBs was under the coordinated effort of INSFOP, whose meetings, though dialogic, were run by religious. Is religious support, at least at the level of the local priest, necessary for legitimation for the CEB members? The tour of Brazilian Bishop Casaldaliga in support of the CEBs while Cardinal Obando y Bravo denounced them at least indicates that the religious leaders thought such hierarchical legitimation was necessary. As Ignacio, another Esteliano CEB member, testified, "Bishops are representatives of Christians and therefore we can't cut ourselves off from them, but right now they are not listening."

With the support of Romero the CEBs flourished. After Romero's assassination, however, his successor, Archbishop Rivera y Damas, under pressures of the Vatican, fellow bishops, the Salvadoran government, and the United States Embassy "began almost immediately to moderate the pastoral line of the diocese." The result was that "the division between the hierarchy and the 'popular church' [deepened]" (Montgomery 1982, 215, 220).

For their part the CEBs have continued in their coordinated action. In 1986 the Third National Assembly of the CEBs met in San Salvador with the authorization of the archdiocese. With the leadership of a few religious, most of the nearly 300 participants were poor and largely rural lay people, representing 100 CEBs all over the country. Included in the meeting was a "political analysis" of the "kidnappings, torture, disappearances, violation of women in military barracks," all of which continued at the hands of the government's "war effort." True to our model's dialogic requisites, openness and consensus, the assembly broke into small groups to discuss the themes: "What is the national reality? and What are the CEBs to do given this reality?" True to the contradictory nature of our model's first and second requisites the CEBs emphasized their freedom from the central authority of Church hierarchy and government. Yet they realized the need for coordination and, perhaps, legitimation and protection. Deciding to "be in communion with the bishops even though they disagree with them," CEBs remained a part of the traditional Church structure, in critical tension with the hierarchy. Their attitude towards the state was less conciliatory, condemning "the government's plan 'United to Build' as "a counterinsurgency program" (Wheaton 1987, 35–38).

Their commitment to openness was reflected in this decision: "We should avoid sectarianism and seek to expand the CEBs, giving wider participation to all persons and work for unity in our communities." The dialogic and consensual format was also maintained in the dynamic of the group discussions: "Everyone was urged to speak; no one could dominate the process; and the discussion had to remain focused on the two themes." The assembly itself was a testimony to the realization of the need for coordination (38).

The repression against the CEBs and their organizers included the expulsion of many religious, the murder of some religious and more lay leaders, the wholesale massacre of towns, and the assassination of Archbishop Romero after he called on the United States to stop sending military aid to the government and invited the men in the army not to obey orders to kill. The priests were accused of "Communist indoctrination" (Prendes 1983, 276, 280, 293). "In the decade beginning in 1972 eleven priests and a seminarian were assassinated. At least sixty priests were expelled or forced into exile" (Montgomery 1982, 218).

Ideology is an important concomitant characteristic for structure in our model of democratic organization for social transformation. The government, for its part, also realized the importance of ideology in its war against the organizing efforts of the CEBs. As a defensive measure, the CEBs were labelled as Communist to justify repression. In using religious faith in an attempt to counter the influence of the CEBs the government took an offensive, encouraging "a wave of North American religious sects." These "charismatic sects" accused the CEBs of being "mere politicians, manipulators of the faith," and taught "that you are serving God just by praying and reading the Bible and not getting involved in anyone's problems." This offensive met with measured success, according to Padre Galdamez's CEB experience. "Many of our members tried to convince themselves of this, abandoning the road the communities had chosen" ([1983] 1986, 60–61).

"Soldiers were coerced into joining these new sects [which would advertise] 'This is a time of crisis! The devil is on the loose, threatening law and order!' " José Napoleon Duarte, who became president, invited an evangelist from such a new sect to preach in the stadium weekly, while people were transported in to hear him for hours on end, driving out of them " 'the demons of Chalatenango and Morazan'—the popular militias" (66–67). And what were these demons, the manipulation of the faith? None other than the "preferential option for the poor" (Prendes 1983, 263), which included the structural analysis of their poverty and organization to improve their lot.

In revolutionary Nicaragua the hierarchy led by Cardinal Obando y Bravo, without the support of the state, has only had the power to verbally assault the CEBs in order to discourage the faithful from participating. Recognizing the importance of clerical leadership, however, the hierarchy has also tried to recall and expel religious who support the CEBs, has gotten more involved in the Church in the countryside and in poor urban areas, making visits and training priests in the seminary who are more reactionary.

GUATEMALA

The national context of the Guatemalan CEBs was fundamentally similar to that of our other Latin American cases. Structural oppression was based on the gross inequitable distribution of land in a country in which the majority of the population subsisted on agricultural produce. Characteristically, 2 percent of the proprietors own 72 percent of the land, with 62 percent of the arable land corresponding to 3 percent of the number of estates with more than 45 hectares. Campesinos unable to subsist on their small plots of land were forced into seasonal labor on large estates. Again this injustice was compounded by the expropriation of peasant-owned lands by agro-industrial projects, hydroelectric projects, and oil and mineral exploration supported by the state, which depended on its military might to repress organized peasant resistance. Geography and ethnicity were contributing factors here too as the Indian population, almost half of the country, lived in the highlands, originally to escape *ladino* (those of Spanish descent) dominance. Mineral explorations also threatened their traditional communal land holdings, and agricultural estates and industries needed their labor power. Again the military power of the state was maintained by U.S. military aid (Sierra Pop 1983, 318, 335).

The control of the external authority, the United States, and the central authorities of the government and Church hierarchy, all stacked up in opposition to the work of the CEBs in organizing the most marginalized to protect their needs and interests. This proved almost fatal for Guatemala's CEBs and verifies the first requisite of our model of democratic organization for social transformation—the need for independence from central and external authorities. As in the other countries studied, the contradictory relationship to authority began with the founding of the CEBs mostly by a progressive clergy influenced by Vatican II, Medellín, and other liberal social teachings of the Church. These religious changed

the traditional pastoral work of the previous years for one which was more in accordance with immediate reality. Many missionaries from remote and inhospitable areas of the country . . . were challenged by the state of misery and exploitation in which the workers lived. Such was the case of religious orders. . . . This situation helped to change the conceptions of Catholic Action [a precursor of the CEB] itself. Priests, assimilating the experience of others in Latin America, began to work in marginal neighbourhoods, factories, unions, considering them as sectors which clearly expressed the present social problematic. (Sierra Pop 1983, 327)

From this new dimension of the Church's social practice, acting out a "preferential option for the poor," was born the CEBs, or what various authors have referred to as the "Church of the Poor" or the "Popular Church."

This is due to a great extent, to the missionaries and parish priests who became involved in the life of the people in a significant way. . . . One priest said: "I seriously considered the ways in which I could approach the people, until I became one of those I came to serve." (Gheerbrand 1970, 200)

Though the majority of the clergy maintained conservative positions, "elements among the clergy were cautiously taking a stand. . . . They ended up getting in contact with guerrillas, whom they supplied with medicines and money" (Latorre Cabal 1969, 81).

Their organizing work, however, is more important for our consideration. As in Nicaragua and El Salvador, the progressive religious set up training and pastoral formation centers, training lay leaders, Delegates of the Word, and developing programs of social consciousness. This resulted in a political consciousness, forming and influencing mass organizations, including "creating cooperatives for the benefit of the peasants" (Sierra Pop 1983, 332–33, 335). "These small and simple experiences encouraged the capacity to make qualitative leaps forward in simple forms of organization and distribution of tasks, that later gave way to more mature forms of political organizations" (Esquivel 1981, 89).

Parallelling our cases in the other national studies of the CEBs, the following account of a Guatemalan CEB illustrates the characteristic movement from religious reflection to organized political confrontation. Two CEB members, Felipe and Elena, indigenous refugees from Guatemala living in sanctuary in Weston Priory, Vermont, described the transformation of their community. It began with "meeting every Sunday afternoon to study the Word of God."

It is from this study that we came to understand that the Word of God was not a simple history of a past time, but what we were living in the present. It is in this manner, that we began to open our eyes little by little, and discover what the reality, *our* reality was. We began to organize more. Our group grew. The numbers grew to more than 125. The first tasks which we began were making home visits to sick people, to people who were in jail, to those married couples who were having matrimonial problems. (Felipe and Elena 1987, 24–25)

From Bible reflection groups that did community outreach, and the study of the Church's social teachings, the work of the CEB became one of organizing and facilitated coordination with other communities.

Each month they had a one day retreat where they met with Catechists from other towns. There they would share experiences about their work in the community. . . . Also, we formed a cooperative in our community in which all the women supported each other in their weaving and the men with their work in the fields. (25)

So organized and critically studying their reality in the light of progressive social teachings, the community's action against political and economic oppression was not far behind.

It was as a consequence of this study that we felt the need to react against the brutal repression that we are suffering under. For us the poor people, the Word of God is a history of liberation not only for the spirit, but also the body. . . . We believe that the people should not be at the service of theology, but that theology should serve the people. We believe that God is the center of liberation and not, as many think, that religion is distant from politics. For us that sounds absurd and alienating. How can you separate the soul from the body? (25–26)

Felipe and Elena also provide us with an illustration of the working of liberation theology and its analysis of their reality.

In Genesis Chapter One, we find that God told us to take care of the land. But one does not see this plan of God happening in Guatemala because the rich people, those that we call Creoles, or those who are not of the indigenous population, and the rich of other countries, such as those represented by the United Fruit Company, have taken over these riches and own the lands that our forefathers, the Mayans, once owned. It is a paradox that in Guatemala, a country rich in cattle, people die of hunger. Meat is exported to the United States, also sugar, bananas, coffee, cocoa, cotton and oil. 85 percent of the fertile land is held by less than 3 percent of the population and [the] other 15 percent of the land which is less fertile is in the hands of more than 85 percent of a very hungry population. (28)

With their sociopolitical awareness came a critique of power relationships, illustrating our model's first requisite of independence from the traditional hierarchical authority of the Church.

However, those who sell the idea that religion and politics are separate, such as the Archbishop whom we had in 1983, Casariego, used to tell us that it was the will of God that we were poor and others had an abundance, so much that they were bursting with their riches. (28)

The testimony of Felipe and Elena illustrates the split between a hierarchy, its priesthood supportive of the status quo, and a progressive clergy, often missionary religious, determined to improve the lot of the poor. Melendez and Richard describe this division in their history of the Church of the Poor:

Then, two lines of action are outlined, almost in totally opposite directions: one, the developmentist–promotionist line [believing that progress will come in the existing capitalist system] . . . the other, through a scientific analysis of reality, making its own the acceptance of social change and development of the worker's consciousness as fundamental to eradicate economic, social and political injustices. (1982, 211)

At its most basic level Felipe and Elena provide an example of this "scientific analysis of reality" in their criticism of the maldistribution of land, inspired by and interspersed with scriptural calls for justice, characteristic of liberation theology.

The result of teaching such analysis, talk of social change, and the organizational effort of the CEBs is that religious are "investigated by the government to determine if they are linked to extremist groups" (Greenhalgh and Gruenke 1982, 27). Repression has been the greatest precisely where peasant lands are threatened by "hydroelectric, agro-industrial projects and oil explorations" and where they are most organized to "demand respect for the workers' rights, the rights to have land and not to be deprived of it" (Sierra Pop 1983, 331–32).

Felipe and Elena describe the resulting repression from the state authorities.

> In order to achieve this liberty, our people have lost their lives and had their precious blood spilt. They have been assassinated. There have been sixteen Catholic priests assassinated in Guatemala. There have been thousands of Cathechists and Christians assassinated. Also there have been twelve Protestant pastors killed. There have been sixty kidnappings and forty-five disappearances. . . . This . . . is happening in the present under our civilian government. . . . In Guatemala, to be a Christian is very dangerous, because Christians are considered to be Communists and subversives. (29)

The CEBs' independence from the central authority of the Church hierarchy is compromised by their dependence in many cases on the leadership of religious and the protection of religious orders. In a country where the CEBs were often cultivated by foreign missionaries (Sierra Pop 1983, 327–28), and where 80 percent of the priests are foreigners (Bermudez 1986, 4), it was undoubtedly a setback to the CEBs when their founders, respectively the Spanish Sacred Heart and the American Maryknoll orders in the Quiche and Huehuetenango provinces, were recalled or expelled, leaving them without priests or sisters. Religious either had to withdraw after the murder of a number of missionaries and other acts of violence (Bermudez 1986, 23), or be expelled when Cardinal Casariego denounced them for collaborating with guerillas (Bermudez 1986, 6).

Again university students, working with religious, provided personnel for outreach. They would give training seminars in poor and marginalized communities, the cursillos de capacitizacion social for CEB formation. The cardinal warned the students, who with missionaries were cultivating the CCSs amongst the Indians, "to stay out of politics" (Bonpane 1983, 13). As with CEPA in Nicaragua, the CCS movement disassociated itself from the hierarchy and declared itself a secular organization and continued its work with the Indians and dialogue with the revolutionary groups. The response in Guatemala of the cardinal along with the superiors of the religious orders was to report the names of the American religious involved to the American ambassador who ordered them expelled "because they could not be protected." The hierarchy branded the CCS leaders as "Communists and antichrists" (Bonpane 1983, 18). As in the other countries studied, this was ironic since the renovation in the Church, of which the CCS was a part, was included in the hierarchy's "anti-Communist strategy." Ideology was also enlisted in this strategy; the hierarchy promoted the popular black Christ of Esquipulas who had been presented as the protector of the counterrevolution of 1954. That counterrevolution had overthrown the socialist and land reform–oriented Arbenz regime with the support of the hierarchy and the U.S. Marines (Berryman 1986, 59).

At the base of the conflict between hierarchy and missionary organizing activity lies the theological and so ideological debate brought to the surface in Vatican II and in the Latin American bishops conferences of Medellín and Puebla. The progressive element, expressed in liberation theology and the pastoral work of the CEBs, argued for the removal of essentialist dualisms, of spirit/matter, earth/heaven, religion/politics.[7] This dualism had traditionally blocked the participation of Christians in the revolutionary process of constructing a more just society (Bonpane 1985, 25). On the other hand the traditionalists, in this case some dominant members of the Guatemalan hierarchy,[8] promoted a reduction of "Christian commitments to individual conversion" (Sierra Pop 1983, 323). As aptly put by Church historian Phillip Berryman, the Church, the landholding oligarchy, and the military were the three pillars of society, and by its traditional theology and pastoral practices the hierarchy cultivated

the day-to-day reinforcement of a fatalistic world view through popular religiosity in which the image of God resembles a celestial hacienda owner. (1986, 59) The Guatemalan hierarchy, in its fear of Marxism and revolution, avoided critiquing the social situation. This silence denoted consent. Despite the new current of Vatican II and Medellin—the hierarchy in its metaphysical and subjective analysis of social problems, did not approach its causes, under the pretext of avoiding the temptation of falling into a marxist analysis and thereby supporting the positions of the guerrilla. Such an ideological position played the role of an ideological function in favour of the State: the respect of the Laws in fact at the disposal of the government and Army. The contributions of national and foreign capital were positively valued, as furnishing jobs to the people and permitting them to produce. (Sierra Pop 1983, 328)

The integrated monist approach, as promulgated by liberation theology, the CEBs, and their precursors, Catholic Action and the cursillos, saw it as el compromiso cristiano to work to change social, economic, political, and religious structures. Their object was to put these structures at the service of the poor, empowering them and so enabling them to participate in the creation of a more just society (Handy 1984, 239–41). Despite the variety of CEBs from country to country, common characteristics include greater lay participation and political involvement in self-direction (Cleary 1985, 104–24), an important requisite of our model of democratic organization for social transformation.

The Guatemalan case illustrates the need for support from a central authority if the challenging democratic organization is to thrive. With external authority (the United States) and the central authorities (of Church and state) antagonistic, the context can prove to be overwhelming and stifle the democratic organization and its attempts at social transformation or at least seriously thwart its efforts. Without the support of the hierarchy, the Church in Guatemala involved in the CEBs suffered brutally from military repression (Greenhalgh and Gruenke 1982). In addition to the killings of dozens of religious and hundreds of lay leaders, whole communities which had been organized were massacred or relocated in military controlled concentrated villages (Handy 1984, 240–57).

From 1978 to 1985 the Guatemalan military, trained, financed, and advised by the United States, killed or "disappeared" 50,000 to 75,000 people, mostly unarmed Indian peasants, destroying 440 rural villages (by the army's own count), creating 100,000 orphans, 20,000 widows, and 150,000 refugees. The new constitution also validates the military decrees that set up the rural concentration camps, "model villages," and puts virtually the entire male population of the Western Highlands, some 900,000, into controlled compulsory "civil patrols." The military has also established outposts in the most remote villages for counterinsurgency (Parenti 1989, 102–3).

As the state recognized the importance of organization, the pattern of repression, as in the other countries studied, usually began with the expulsion of missionary religious, the recall of progressive clergy, and the murder of local organizers. Anthropologic field workers at the time verified the organizing activities and changes brought about in the Guatemalan Indian communities by Catholic Action and cursillos: founding of CEBs and the work of coordinating with other villages concerning common problems. The Guatemalan government and military attempted to destroy village autonomy and gain control over the countryside through their program of selected assassination, massacres, and village relocation (Handy 1984, 241–43, 25–61). The military having successfully intimidated religious in the department of El Quiche, only one conservative priest placed there by the cardinal kept his church open (Black 1984, 132–33). The Jesuits, who were largely responsible for religious organization in the department, withdrew their priests, "citing 'a climate of insecurity which prevents any kind of evangelical or pastoral work' " (243).

As in our other cases, ideology, concomitant to structural change in our model, was also used in the Guatemalan repression. Not only were lay leaders of cooperatives and prayer groups targeted, but so too was the Catholic Church, the antagonists labelling them as "Marxist inspired" and "Communists" (242). Recognizing the importance of ideology, the presidency of Rios Montt made an ideological push to encourage conversion away from Catholicism and to Evangelical Protestant sects which appealed "to individuality and subservience to earthly and heavenly authority."[9] Colonel Robert Matta, commander of the military region of El Quiche, declared in 1982, "We make no distinction between the Catholic Church and the Communist subversives." Montt, himself a born-again Pentecostal, preached the values of his new-found faith in weekly national sermons and encouraged sects, such as Francisco Bache's Assembly of God in El Quiche, which taught, "He who resists authority is resisting that which has been established by God" (Black 1984, 130–34).

The situation of the Guatemalan CEBs are, however, further complicated by the ethnic variable, since much of the organizing effort had been done among highland Mayan Indians and political and economic power is held by the ladinos (Handy 1984, 242). Montt's attempt at building up Guatemalan nationalism, *Guatemalidad*, "as a doctrine opposed to international communism" (Black 1984, 131) was in reality an attempt to further destroy the indigenous culture of the Indians (Handy 1984, 256–60). As Montt's defense minister declared, "We must do away with the words 'indigenous' and 'Indian.' Our mission requires the integration of all Guatemalans" (Black 1984, 131). The result of such a policy has been genocide of the Indian community (Sierra Pop 1983, 340).

That this repression was done in the name of anticommunism (Bermudez 1985, 46–54) illustrates the use of ideology by the central authorities of hierarchy and government to maintain their power in the face of the challenge posed by democratic organization. As in other Latin American countries, it is one of the great ironies of the CEBs that their precursors in Guatemala, Catholic Action (Handy 1984, 238) and the cursillos (Bonpane 1983, 12), were originally cultivated to combat Marxism among the populace. Archbishop Rossell of Guatemala had even explicitly encouraged Catholic Action by calling it "one of the greatest comforts in those hours of enormous distress in the presence of Marxist advance that invaded everything." Catholic Action was not originally cultivated for the political empowerment of the Indians but rather to delay the Indian rebellion, as Rossell aptly put it, by "encouraging the feeling of 'Christian resignation' among the poor." He warned, "Today [the Indian population] is a tame and long suffering lamb, but it is very easy to turn it into a cruel wolf, or a ravenous lion, or a poisonous snake" (Handy 1984, 238). Catholic Action was also responsible for heightening unrest amongst the villages in opposition to Arbenz's socialist reforms, prior to that government's overthrow in 1954. Yet scarcely over a decade later the cursillos and Catholic Action were responsible for developing local autonomous organizations, cooperatives, dialogue on social and economic concerns, encouraging local political parties that reflected peasant concerns, and promoting literacy (Handy 1984, 239–40).

Anthropologist Kay Warren's work illustrates the second characteristic of our model, the need for coordination, as it was affected in the Guatemalan case. Her study of Catholic Action amongst the highland Indians concludes that it not only " 'began to forge a more active Indian population' but also inspired an increased sense of connection with other neighbouring villages and their common problems," rejecting ladino dominance (Handy 1984, 241). Before the end of the 1960s religious missionaries were being expelled for their organizing activities and a decade later the list of religious and trained lay leaders murdered by military and paramilitary groups began to grow (Handy 1984, 242–44; Bermudez 1986; Black 1984; Greenhalgh and Greunke 1982).

That the founding religious, representing the central religious authority, also coordinated the various communities illustrates the contradictory nature of the change agent between our model's first and second characteristics: freedom from central authority and the need for coordination. The CEBs were not independent of the central authority since they were the product of religious orders who also coordinated the various CEBs. It also highlights a fundamental political naïvety of the Church at the time. It intended the cooperative movement and Catholic Action to "improve local social and economic conditions without challenging the status quo" (Handy 1984, 242). Yet any initiatives like these would bring the organized community into conflict with the traditional social, economic, and political powers. Because of its traditional passivist role, supportive of the status quo, the Church was not prepared for the conflict and bloodshed that would result.

The dominant members of the hierarchy in Guatemala secured their own position by condemning the cursillos and the CEBs, and by supporting Montt (Bonpane 1980, 184–86). With the absence of religious leadership and a hierarchy allied with the government, the central support for the CEBs was gone and they were persecuted ruthlessly. Their continued existence was only possible in a clandestine fashion. However, now that the conservative Cardinal Casariego has been replaced, the hierarchy has taken more of a denunciatory stand toward the government (Handy 1984, 271).

That the CEBs have continued at all without the support of any central authority testifies to the empowerment of democratic organization for social transformation once the process has been set in motion. If this were not the case, the CEBs and their organizing activity would vanish with the absence of their religious leadership. But with the organizational skills learned, leadership shared in a dialogic and consensual manner, the strength of the organization did not rest solely on a few leaders who could be eliminated but rather in the organizational process itself as outlined in the requisites of our model—making the community itself the agency of change. The work in the CEBs was taken over by the lay leaders who had been trained by religious, the Delegates of the Word, whose task was extremely risky since any meeting, including religious, could be considered subversive and result in persecution and death (Bermudez 1986, 23–51).

However, this is a limited verification of their independence, for as Sierra Pop notes, the continued functioning of the CEBs, in small clandestine meetings, "oriented to prevent the disappearance of priests and monks and nuns" (1983, 345) indicates the importance of the leadership of religious. Here, as in the El Salvadoran and Nicaraguan cases, the first requisite of our model—independence from the central authority—is compromised by dependence on religious leaders for the very establishment of the CEBs. Furthermore, the difficulties of the CEBs to continue their work in Guatemala attests more to the importance of the overriding context of political repression and government policies of genocide.

What of this repression in the name of anticommunism, and does it have any bearing on our model? The cursillos, although designed to combat communism, became in the hands of missionary religious tools for social analysis of a community's ills, at times including Marxist analysis (Bonpane 1985, 31–32). The question then for our model arises, If Marxist analysis was used, was it used as a means of revolutionary indoctrination or as a means of social analysis, providing tools to a people which would enable them to better understand and improve their situation? This is not to argue that all CEBs employed Marxist analysis of their social situation. Rather the evidence points to the contrary, that the CEBs and their precursors were established to improve the conditions of the poor as an alternative to Marxism or the feared red spectre of communism. According to Juan Carlos Scannone's study of the Church in Latin America, the majority of the priests leading the CEBs practiced a

l·beration theology predominantly concerned with being a theology of popular pastoral activity, [which] underlines the values of popular culture, the . . . historical roots of the current liberation process, and an openness of this process to a qualitatively new society that would be neither capitalist nor Marxist. (Montgomery 1982, 210)

A smaller minority emphasized

a liberation theology predominantly influenced by Marxist categories and methodology in its concern to analyze and transform reality . . . emphasizing social criticism of injustice, ethico-prophetical denunciation, and identification with the poor and oppressed. (210)

But even these, according to a participating priest, "use 'the analysis of Marx because it is objective and scientific. But we are not Marxists. We cannot understand Marx as a religion because we are Christians' " (210).

However, any attempt to improve the lot of the poor involved coordinated action, the formation of cooperatives and unions in order to secure land and improve workers' rights. Such attempts disturbed the status quo and one of the more acceptable reasons for repression was in the name of anticommunism.

The labels of "Communist" and "Marxist inspired" were liberally used against the peasant cooperatives (Handy 1984, 242), founded by Catholic Action and the cursillos. One student put on the death list of *La Mano Blanca*, the right-wing death squad, was accused of being a Communist. A member of the squad testified, "I know he's a communist because I heard him say he would give his life for the poor" (Bonpane 1985, 29). The fact that not only Maryknoll missionaries, of which Bonpane was one, were expelled from Guatemala, but that the Jesuits also had to leave for fear of their lives and that cooperative political and economic actions by Indians were denounced as Marxist indicates what others have claimed: Political repression and military extermination became the means of refusing power to an increasingly organized and politically active formerly passive population (Bermudez 1986, 46; Handy 1984, 242). The evidence reviewed indicates that the Marxist analysis, where it was employed in the CEBs, was not used in a doctrinaire fashion, but rather in accordance with our model—dialogically and consensually. In short, anticommunism was a label used to thwart the social transformation initiated by the democratic organization of the CEBs.

Anthropologist Douglas Brintall provides an example of how the CEBs illustrate our model's democratic organization for social transformation. In Aguacatan, the Indians involved in Catholic Action were able to wrest control of the local political parties from the ladinos. However, the overriding context of political repression, particularly of the Indian population, seriously inhibited the model's effects: When an Indian was elected mayor the local ladino military commissioner used a minor dispute to bring down the punishment of the army on the Indian people. In another case a Spanish priest organized a local Indian cooperative. When the cooperative began to impinge on local ladino profits the papal nuncio was pressured to remove the priest from his post (Handy 1984, 241–42). Again the central authority, in the former case the state, in the latter the Church hierarchy, inhibited the democratic organization's ability to function.

There is evidence in these instances not only of the importance of authority but also of the other three requisites of our model. The cultivation of self-esteem in members, essential for the dialogic characteristic of the model's requisites of openness and consensus, is illustrated in the following. Commenting on the change among the Indians because of the organizational work of the cursillos, "one long-time Guatemalan resident remarked: I am astounded at the way the Indians talk now. . . . When I arrived they used to bow before the white man. Now they want to discuss their 'oppression' " (240). Warren also commented on the effect of Catholic Action:

By stressing education that often entailed leaving the village temporarily, Catholic Action fostered a group of young people who not only rejected ladino dominance and felt restricted by the lack of opportunity in the village, but also eventually gained the support of many village elders. Elders reacted positively to Indian youth who "do not permit ladinos to bother them, now they speak out and give opinions, now that they have ideas and have studied. They know some of the laws and they will not allow ladinos to do something bad in the municipal government." (Handy 1984, 240)

Warren found that Catholic Action not only " 'began to forge a more active Indian population' but also inspired an increased sense of connection with other neighbouring villages and their common problems" (240). As in our model, coordination of this sort is an essential requisite for social transformation and effective opposition to oppression. The Guatemalan regime recognized this threat to their authority, trying to break up coordinated activity in its "scheme for forcing highland peasants to abandon their scattered communities and to relocate in concentrated villages the military could more easily control" (256–57).

The Guatemalan instance also shows the importance of the Indian ethnic variable. Ladino dominance of the Indian population as part of the larger social context indicates the importance of the context in enabling the democratic organization and its attempts at social transformation to work. If the larger social context does not support or at least allow the democratic organization to function, any attempts at social transformation are severely restricted. Again an overwhelming factor is authority and its use. The Church hierarchy's withdrawal of support for the cursillos and labelling them as "Communist," and "antichrists" gave legitimation to the government's widespread persecution of any organization of the poor.

Let us turn our attention now to Brazil to study this problem of authority and the tools of social analysis in the CEBs and in the education of the masses in another context. In contrast to Guatemala, in Brazil, the authority—the Church hierarchy—explicitly supported and set out to cultivate the CEBs and the mass popular-education campaign.

BRAZIL

As with the Central American countries studied, the CEBs in Brazil had roots which pre-existed Vatican II, again most notably Catholic Action and its accompanying anticommunism. But as with the other cases we have studied, it was Medellín, the "preferential option for the poor," and the desire to reach out to the previously unattended flock that gave impetus for the flourishing of the CEBs. That the CEBs and their precursors were clerical in origin is again reaffirmed, including the influence of foreign-educated missionaries employing the benefits of social science, in particular sociological analysis (Barbe 1987, 94, 19). What is particular about the Brazilian case which furthers our comparative analysis was the support of the hierarchy for the CEBs.

The shortage of priests typical to Latin American countries is acute in Brazil, the largest Catholic country. With only one priest to every thousand parishioners, the CEBs were seen as an indispensable means of tending the flock. So prolific had the CEBs become that one estimate gave their number as 80,000 in Brazil (Mainwaring 1988). They became indispensable as part of the planning and administration of parish life (Ribeiro de Oliveira 1988).

What does this mean concerning the first characteristic of our model, the relation to authority?

Being cultivated and supported by the hierarchy had a mixed effect on the CEBs. As in our other cases studied, trying to follow the directives of the councils to better serve the poor and improve their living situation entailed conflict with the military and government authorities. As in all Latin American countries, the hierarchy traditionally supported the government and military. However, the Brazilian hierarchy, led by progressive bishops, reacted differently than in Guatemala where the hierarchy continued to associate with the government and military—giving ideological support to the repression of the CEBs, denouncing leaders to the authorities as Communists. In Brazil the hierarchy distanced themselves from the government and military and courageously defended the work of the CEBs including their land claims (Barbe 1987). However, with the ending of the military regime in Brazil and the desire of the hierarchy to better control and integrate the CEBs with the rest of parish life, a more recent crisis in authority resulted (Ribeiro de Oliveira 1988). It brings to question the future of the CEBs, not only in Brazil but in the rest of Latin America as well.

Let us first consider again the relationship of ideology and structure in our model as it presents itself in the Brazilian case. In our model, ideology is a concomitant requisite with structure in democratic organization for social transformation. Again case studies of CEBs in Brazil display the salient feature of contrasting their liberation ideology with that of the traditional scholastic theology and the Calvinist theology of individual salvation. The liberation theology of the CEBs is characterized by a community aspect, immediacy of the reign of God, and the ability of people working together to construct the kingdom of justice by organized action to improve the lot of its members.

Cecilia Madriz, in her comparison of the CEBs and Pentecostal churches in Brazil, contrasts their ideology and resulting actions. Examining their theology and practices, Madriz concludes that the Pentecostal churches promulgated a theology/ideology which emphasized the individual, focusing on personal characteristics such as work habits to improve one's lot in life and to insure one's salvation; salvation being very much a phenomenon of the world to come or after death. The CEBs, on the other hand, with their liberation theology and organization of the community, prepared their members for collective action on political, economic, and social concerns as these were considered integral to building up the Kingdom of God in this life (1988).

Barbe, in his study of the CEBs in the diocese of São Paulo, focuses on their collective action as their defining characteristic (1987, 100). It is here that ideology and practice, referred to as praxis by various Latin American social scientists (Le Boterf 1981; Arroyo and Medina 1982; Fals-Borda 1978), or orthopraxis by liberation theologians (Cleary 1985, 94), come together in the life of the CEB. The religious cultural context, the language of faith, is still the medium of discourse but now the focus is on selected scriptural passages and an interpretation encouraging collective action. The traditional Church authorities of Scripture, papal social encyclicals, and religious are now seen as giving legitimation to collective action for social justice in the face of poverty and oppression. A Brazilian missionary involved in the CEBs provides an illustration:

Still today, as in the age of Gideon, we have to destroy the altars of false gods where human energies are destroyed under Satan's sun: namely, the unjust laws and social structures that turn the human being into a machine for production, instead of being a creature in the image of God made to love and be loved. It is certain that prayer, the celebration of the faith, biblical and theological study, and nourishment by the sacraments are indispensable to gospel energy, as we have insisted. But we must never forget that only action can verify whether or not prayer is authentic: "Not those who say 'Lord, Lord' . . ." (Mt.7:21). People can pray together for twenty years side by side in the same church and never have a disagreement. But on the day when they begin to act together, everything starts to change. That is when we see whether the charity that "bears all things, hopes all things, believes all things, endures all things" (1 Cor. 13:7) will win out over our egotism and allow us to work together. That is the decisive moment when a base community is born. (Barbe 1987, 100)

The application of social science to the particular historical context is crucial in understanding the ideology of liberation theology and its relation to structure in making the CEBs effective. This ideology is the motivating force behind the structure of the CEBs fulfilling the requisites of coordination, openness, and consensus in our model. In a very real sense ethnographic research is conducted to determine the community's needs and means of expression, psychological tools are employed to develop the self-esteem of the community members, and sociological tools of dialogue and consensus for organization building are used to mobilize and empower participants. As with Smutko's Nicaraguan case—employing anthropology in developing a pastoral approach to CEB formation with the Indian population in northeastern Nicaragua—so too is it applied in Brazil where ethnographic sensitivity allows the missionary, or educator in the case of the mass literacy campaigns, to integrate himself into the community.

On this application of the social sciences in liberation theology to the work of the CEBs in Brazil, Barbe elaborates:

Theology is nothing but organized discourse on the data of faith. . . . "Will not the simple gospel be enough?" Actually, no. Every age is different and the course of time brings new problems at every moment. The questions of an industrial society have their own special character; so do the Middle Ages, so do those of the third world. . . . We do not have the option of being pre-Marxist, pre-Nietzscheans, pre-Freudians. So in every age we have to reorganize the data of the faith so that they will really be an answer to the problems of a contemporary human being. . . . We must . . . ask the right questions about the "practice." . . . So our reason will make use of all the scientific means at our disposal—philosophy, philology, economics, history, sociology—to render our religious discourse more penetrating, more complete, more organized . . . in particular with sociology. (18–19)

So it is not that liberation theology or the CEBs have merely substituted a Marxist ideology for a traditionally passive scholastic theology, though that is always a danger. Rather, by applying the social sciences to the life of the community the CEBs seek to improve the life of their members. That application and analysis of the social sciences is no more Marxist than the social sciences are. Applying social science, they also make use of Marx's contribution to social analysis, as they would make use of Maslow in realizing the importance of developing self-esteem.

This application of the social sciences is precisely what the CEBs do. Their religious practices provide them with a structure—"the Church is their sole place for meeting"—and an ideology—"the anticipation of a new world within societies in the process of change." Thus, in the relationship of ideology and structure, the ideology provides "the principal motivation" for "a gigantic *restructuring*" of society, one based in "community" (88, 89, 96).

Indeed much of the methodology in the formation of the CEBs and in liberation theology, employing the social sciences, participates in the *au courant* debates and methodological issues of the social sciences, for example, the relationship between theory and practice. Latin American social scientists such as Marcos Arruda consider it an integral part of their study to work side by side at the jobs of poor factory workers in Brazil. Furthermore social scientists and theologians in the Latin American context refer to each other's work in an interdisciplinary fashion, a dialectic of social ethics and social sciences. That these distinctions between science and religion, politics and education are not as clearly defined in Latin American studies is due to the historical context of a Church and state which have been integrated and mutually supportive.

All religion is political. This is true not only in the CEBs but in the traditional Catholic Church urging suffering compliance for a reward in heaven. Though Pentecostals do not all monolithically accept the status quo (Mainwaring 1989), it is true of the fundamentalist Pentecostal sects, such as Rios Montt's, which foster an acceptance of the status quo or, as seen in Madriz's study, put the responsibility for poverty on the work habits of the individual. This traditional Catholic and Calvinist religiosity is political, and also psychological and economic, but I would argue it is to the disadvantage of the poor, since no organizational, structural basis is given for improving the lot of the most disenfranchised in society other than working hard within a system which is exploiting their labor.

The relationship between ideology and structure is of course dialectic. The origin of the CEBs and their precursors, the cursillos and Catholic Action, cooperatives and the Delegates of the Word, lies with the religious who were educated in the social sciences as well as theology. Brazilian educator Paulo Freire of the Catholic University of São Paulo describes how these new studies provided a meaning to their experience of the wealth of the first world in North America, Europe, or developed parts of third world cities, while pursuing their education. This was juxtaposed to their pastoral activities amongst the poorest, most exploited, and disenfranchised peoples in the third world. Their ideological background, a Christian vision of justice, and analytic tools of social science gave meaning to their experience of structures of wealth and poverty or "institutionalized violence." Vatican II, Medellín, and Puebla gave further impetus and direction, validating the work of religious in such precursors as the cursillos and Catholic Action, encouraging a "preferential option for the poor" and the application of social sciences to better their lot through the organization of communities and education for the training of leaders (Paulo Freire, interview with the author 17 July 1987). The founding religious were motivated by an ideology of liberation and armed with the knowledge of the necessity of providing a structure to enable change—that organization is essential to empowerment.

The missionary Barbe provides an account of how this knowledge was applied in a six-stage methodology in the creation of CEBs in the diocese of São Paulo. The first is "living together." The religious "embrace the cause of the oppressed, break with one's position in the ruling class, 'live with' even in material circumstances if in any way possible as regards one's quarters, daily work, and so on" ([1982] 1987, 95).

This is similar to Freire's concept of "class suicide," which, he argues, only happens on an individual basis (1987). Thus, the agent of change is to throw his lot in with the community, to be at the service of the community's self-determined needs. The other stages in Barbe's analysis of CEB formation in Brazil likewise can be applied to educators and social-science researchers in Latin America who are concerned with praxis: a consciously directed research practice which expresses their solidarity with the poor whom they are studying and whom they hope to benefit (Le Boterf 1981; Arroyo and Medina 1982; Fals-Borda 1978).

Barbe's second stage is to "always start with the people's traditions" (1987, 95). Paralleling the cases of the CEBs in the other countries we have studied, CEB building is community building. Going door to door in one's neighborhood, a priest organizing a CEB might use the "religious tradition . . . of the Rosary, a casa em casa [where] everybody comes, and it is a chance for the neighbors in the same street to meet each other or to deepen a passing acquaintance" (95–96). This is the fundamental method used by the CEBs in initiating our model's characteristics, especially coordination, at the most basic level of the barrio. This door-to-door technique is particularly important in new barrios made up of migrants to urban areas. By drawing on traditional religious practices and invigorating them with new meaning in a community setting, the CEB fosters familiarity among members, necessary for democratic organization, as well as providing an ideological vision of how things should be (96). In Nicaragua, the weekly Stations of the Cross done in procession through the town fulfilled a similar function. Drawing from neighborhoods as the procession proceeded, traditional prayers were intermingled with an interpretation of Nicaragua as the Christ crucified by the terrorist acts of the contras, paid soldiers, not in this instance of the Roman Empire but of the American (Journal Entry 414, 6 September 1985).

True to our model's requisites of openness and consensus, in Barbe's third stage of CEB development the self-worth of each individual and their participation in the self-direction of the group is cultivated by giving a voice to participants, having each tell what happened to them that day or week, describing their family, and telling their story or past. As Barbe describes it:

That is why each base community is founded through a gentle and gradual pedagogy, which teaches the humble once again to listen to each other and speak to each other *in community;* to *give worth* to what they have to say as they express themselves to each other. (97)

Included in this recognition of the self-worth of each individual and his/her rights is an openness to the participant's concerns and a challenge to the oppression of the existing social structure in guided questions: " 'If you had the chance, what would you want to get before everything else for yourself and your children?' . . . and . . . 'If you could, how would you change the *barrio* [neighborhood] . . . your work area, the whole factory?' " (98–99). Answers are guided by an ideology of liberation: studying the gospel to see how Jesus sided with the poor and worked against oppression is a part of these questions seeking a solution. Barbe describes a typical CEB meeting:

1. song or initial prayer, after the usual greeting;
2. reading a text from the Bible;
3. storytelling by the participants on one of the general themes [described in the above guide questions] . . . ;
4. discussion of problems that have been discovered during the meeting, or an effort to solve an urgent question that has come up in the *barrio;*
5. prayer and final song. (99)

Though varying from the Guatemalan cursillos or Nicaraguan meetings (and Barbe states that even in the diocese of his study they varied) the format is generally the same: getting acquainted, studying scripture, studying local problems, and seeking a solution. There is no mention of Marxist analysis here and yet social critique follows in discussing the barrio's problems.

For Barbe the fourth stage in the development of the CEB, "acting together," is the essential characteristic of the CEB. From reconstructing the slum dwelling of a widowed mother of eleven against the laws of the town council, to land claims for a barrio, Barbe describes the actions of the CEBs and the inevitable division of labor according to the talents of the participants: organizer, preacher, treasurer, politician (99–105). True to our model of democratic organization, to maintain the character of consensus Barbe warns that the CEB must militate against those with specialized tasks becoming the new authorities rather than facilitating consensus.

There is a real danger of turning the base community into a mini-parish, and the layperson who takes on some ministry into a mini-curé. This danger has not always been avoided. What makes all the difference is the orientation to mission right from the beginning. . . . The transformation of the world so that love is possible. . . . The vision. (102)

Again we see that not only are the structural means necessary to facilitate consensus, but the membership and especially leaders are motivated by a vision of a just society and must adhere to an ideology which requires egalitarian participation of the full membership. In this way the community itself becomes the agency of change, rather than the initial missionary or religious, or trained lay leader, remaining or becoming the directive change agent.

The second requisite of our model of democratic organization for successful social transformation also involves coordination with other individuals and groups striving for the same social change. As in our other national cases, this inevitably predisposed CEB membership to an openness to other revolutionary organizations and an interface of membership. In the CEB's movement to collective action, Barbe describes that after community has been formed on a religious basis, the motivated membership will variously participate in political, unionist, and even militant "popular movements" and bring their concerns and struggles back to the community for discussion—characteristic of our model's requisites of openness and consensus.

Barbe argues that this activity in the political realm is a "consequence" of the members being in a political world and not the "essence" of the CEBs which he says is religious (105–6). However, this retreat in the last moment to a defensive dualist position belies the monist contention in liberation theology and pedagogy that in reality the political and religious, education and politics, science and religious belief, the Kingdom of God to come and the struggles for justice in this world, cannot be separated. As in Randall's account of CEB participation in Managua, the community of faith provided the support necessary in making individual decisions for political and even militant action.

With the end of military rule in Brazil a new crisis has ensued for the CEBs, one which brings to the fore our model's first characteristic, the relation with central authority. The support of the bishops has been a mixed blessing. Under their encouragement the CEBs have flourished (Mainwaring 1986, 109). However, with the end of the dictatorship, the worst oppression has disappeared. At first many of the bishops had welcomed the military coup of 1964 as saving Brazil from communism, and then moved to a position of defending the CEBs (Freire, interview with the author 17 July 1987). However, with the removal of the military dictatorship, the bishops more recently are striving to bring in the reins on the CEBs. This move to bring them under control and integrate their necessary function into the existing parish structure is to avoid a duplication of Church structure—a Church of the poor (CEBs) as separate from the Church of the rich (the diocesan cathedral)—and a challenge to the authority of the bishop (Ribeiro de Oliveira 1988).

This was not a concern of the episcopate before because of the differing context of the time. Reformed by Vatican II and Medellín they sought to reach the unattended masses and the CEBs were an effective means of doing so. Because of the common enemy that the military dictatorship came to be, the hierarchy defended the organizational work of the CEBs. But now that the CEBs have developed into a strong viable entity, their independence and ability to challenge government and hierarchy appears to be unsettling, at least to the conservative bishops who are increasingly gaining control of the Brazilian National Bishops Conference and the Latin American Bishops Conference because of the appointments of a conservative Pope John Paul II (Lernoux 1989).

Though not brutally oppressed as in Guatemala, or deprecative of the CEBs as in Nicaragua, the hierarchy, as in El Salvador, by seeking to control the CEBs, brings to the fore the issue of authority. Can the CEBs function as a truly democratic organization engaged in social transformation when their very history, their social context, the institution of which they are part, seeks to control and limit their autonomy? The Catholic Church still is hierarchical and the CEBs flourished during the two most progressive papacies. Through episcopal nominations and pressure, the current papacy has effectively curtailed the growth of the popular Church and the CEBs (Lernoux 1989). Mainwaring captures the contradiction of the CEBs within an authoritarian Church.

Grassroots movements alone were not, however, responsible for the Church's transformation. On the contrary, without support from the hierarchy these movements could not have transformed the Church. The transformation process was dialectical.

. . . Given the hierarchical structure of the Catholic Church, movements not supported by the bishops remain relatively isolated and are incapable of changing the thrust of the institution's weight. (1986, 15)

Obviously the ideal democratic organization does not exist as does not the ideal CEB. Nor (when approximations of the ideal exist) do they occur in a vacuum, but rather in a particular economic, political, and social context, and all the constraints that such a context entails. It was due to a lack of clerical leadership and later repression that the Church cultivated and prioritized the CEBs. A central authority cultivating an independent organization, because of the central authority's inability to reach the masses under its control, is a rare instance of a central authority creating an organization which could challenge its own power structure. It is another fundamental contradiction in our case studies: emphasizing "participatory, egalitarian values" in "a traditionally elitist society" (Mainwaring 1986, 15, 103–108, 179). It is a rare instance that an organization free of both state control and a hierarchical central authority exists, and that it exists within the context of a limited repression; limited because of the protection of that hierarchy. In Brazil the Church hierarchy, regarded by the state as a legitimate authority to be heeded, was able to protect the CEBs and their organizing activity from the worst repression which befell the CEBs in Guatemala and El Salvador. In these countries the state, in particular the presidency, finding an alternative in the Protestant Pentecostals, argued that the Catholic Church was dispensable.

In trying to discover the salient features of a democratic organization for social transformation it is important to extend the comparative analysis beyond other CEBs, so the requisites for such an organization can be seen in a form other than the religious one. In differing contexts one is able to isolate the recurrent necessary patterns that bare out the hypothesis: in this case the requisite characteristics of a democratic organization for social transformation. Otherwise what might be considered necessary for the theoretical model might be the secondary characteristics or particular form in which the requisite is expressed in a particular case study, a descriptive model. This will enable us to make broader generalizations from our model.

For this reason we turn now to the mass popular-education campaign in Brazil for another example of an attempt at employing democratic organization for social transformation within the constraints of a larger undemocratic social context. This will be followed by the post-Triumph Nicaraguan literacy campaign and popular education, providing another case of democratized education for analysis and comparison to our model.

8

Mass Education as Democratic Process

INTRODUCTION

There has been a good deal written regarding the educational process in revolutionary Nicaragua. An examination of the content of the new curriculum and texts illustrate the attempt to inform the "new Nicaraguan." A pre-Triumph content which showed the American-funded Alliance for Progress as the savior of Nicaragua's development has been changed for one which shows the exploitation: first of the Indians by the Spaniards and then of Nicaraguan peasants by agricultural elites in collaboration with American corporations and Anastasio Somoza's military dictatorship.

This change in history-telling can hardly be called transformative in the sense of our model of democratic organization. A change in content is not the essence of liberation theology or of revolutionary pedagogy. If it is to be revolutionary in the transformative sense of empowerment of previously illiterate and disenfranchised people, if it is to give them a voice in their own self-direction, then it must provide a methodology whereby they tell and make their own history. It must be a process which provides them with the tools of analysis, enabling them to write and speak of their own situation and re-create it by participating in the democratic process. This is the fundamental meaning of literacy and education and its part in the democratic process. As Paulo Freire states:

I agreed with Mannheim that "as democratic processes become widespread, it becomes more and more difficult to permit the masses to remain in a state of ignorance." Mannheim would not restrict his definition of ignorance to illiteracy, but would include the masses' lack of experience at participating and intervening in the historical process. (1973, 41)

If it is merely a replacement of authorities, a pro-American for a pro-revolutionary Sandinista interpretation of their history, then is the educational process in any manner empowering? It may be if it gives a more accurate account of the history of the nation. However, unless the educational process is dialogic and listens at least as much as it provides tools, then it can be accused of being simply another ideological interpretation. For as Freire, Bourdieu, Willis, and Bowles and Gintis have argued, all education is political, and at worst a means of manipulation, perpetuating and promoting particular class interests (Freire 1970; Bourdieu 1977; Bowles and Gintis 1976; Willis 1977).

BRAZIL'S POPULAR EDUCATION

Since so much of the change in education in Latin America, and particularly in Nicaragua, refers to the work of Paulo Freire in Brazil, before turning to the literacy campaign and new education in revolutionary Nicaragua I will look at the mass popular-education campaign in Brazil and Freire's work. How do those campaigns measure up to the ideals of democratic education as proposed in Freire's methodology and how does that relate to our model of democratic organization for social transformation?

Freire claims that his is not a "methodology" but a process (1985, 71). Although it does provide a method for educating we must at least recognize the distinction that he makes for the important emphasis it places on the actual context of the education and how the process is constantly re-created in every unique situation by the participants. Rather than lose sight of the reality of the Brazilian educational campaign, let us begin with that rather than the theory. I will consider the theory later, for as we have seen with our model, an ideal theoretical construction, though helpful in the analysis of a situation and for prediction, does not describe the complexity of the historical reality.

José Marins, one of the most quoted theologians in the development of the CEBs and author of guidebooks for their formation, refers to three convergent forces in the origins of the CEBs in Brazil:

1. evangelizing the community, expressing the word of God in a language and a catechesis which could reach the often neglected masses;

2. the *Movimiento Educacao de Base*, (Base Education Movement, MEB), which tried to develop a popular education campaign to reach the illiterate masses;

3. the national plans of the hierarchy for pastoral renovation, very much in keeping with the directives of Pope John XXIII and Vatican II. (1975, 26)

A distinctive feature here from the CEB cases we have so far studied in other countries is the MEB: popular education as integral to the outreach of the Church in the Brazilian CEBs.

The MEB, 1961–65, was inaugurated and coordinated by the Brazilian National Bishops Conference, a Catholic Church hierarchy. The majority of the movement was made up of members of Catholic Action and the Catholic University Youth (Wanderly 1984, 64). Wanderly's study discusses the MEB's objectives and practices for transformation of Brazilian economic, political, cultural, and social life and the resulting tendencies and conflicts. Notable among its economic objectives was to break underdevelopment by structural reforms which would make communities self-sufficient. This structural reform and desire for community self-sufficiency are indicative of the first requisite of our model of democratic organization for social transformation—independence from a central and external authority.

The MEB hoped to bring about structural reform by making the masses literate, organizing them into groups and workers' associations, and training leaders within the community that would acquire political power and challenge existing structures. Culturally this meant a base education, *concientização* (conscientization), which valued the masses' own oral tradition and cultivated self-worth (Wanderly 1984, 39). A precursor to the CEBs in Brazil, the MEB,

like Paulo Freire, developed an ideal of education as an exchange between teacher and learner, anticipating the philosophy developed later by the popular Church. The good pedagogue should start from the popular world view, which the teacher must learn from the masses. "Education, as we understand it, must be realized through dialogue." Finally, MEB helped introduce the belief that a fundamental goal of Christian faith is the full realization of all people. The movement emphasized the importance of encouraging greater self-respect among the poor. (Mainwaring 1986, 67)

This pedagogy of the MEB characterizes the openness of our model, since it begins with the experience of the learner. It also characterizes the requisite consensus through dialogue and the realization of the self-worth of each individual. It illustrates as well the ideological concomitants to these third and fourth requisites of our model in the recognition of the value of each individual and his/her rights and self-direction by the full participation of all members.

In practice the MEB was somewhat similar to CEPA in Nicaragua, the work of the CEBs in El Salvador, and Catholic Action and CCS in Guatemala. It included teaching new agricultural techniques and experimenting with cooperatives, developing unions, political radio programs, projects to promote popular culture and many meetings to encourage community, all of which characterize our model's second requisite, the need to coordinate effort. Wanderly describes the "tendencies" resulting from the MEB's efforts as necessitating the defense of the worker and the community, the creation of Popular Action whose goal was political influence and the encouragement of popular local power and the promotion of social equality (1984, 40). Again this fostering of local power characterizes our model's relationship to authority—the right to self-determination. The promotion of social equality again characterizes the ideological concomitants of openness and consensus—respectively the self-worth of each individual and self-direction by the full participation of all members.

What Wanderly describes as the resulting conflicts are of interest to our study because they illustrate the contradictory nature of the relationship of the democratic organization for social change with the central authority. In this case the contradiction lies between the MEB and the Church hierarchy who founded it. Wanderly found that only a few agents and educating teams of the MEB actually comprehended the "productive relations . . . in terms of bourgeois economics" (40). Despite the MEB's design, the grass roots participants did not see their problem in terms of Marxist analysis, however, their existential problem still expressed itself in the need for land for sustenance, and therefore land reform.

Wanderly describes the conflicts which resulted from property owners who with the traditional politically powerful whose authority was questioned were opposed to the MEB and its organizational efforts to empower the previously disenfranchised. It was in this context, the success of the MEB, that Freire, the principal proponent of popular education (36–40), was exiled from Brazil as a result of the reactionary military coup of 1964. This coup was at first welcomed by the Catholic right, the majority of the hierarchy of the Church, as a triumph against communism. The MEB also illustrates the contradictory position of the agents of change, the reform-minded bishops, educators, and religious who were situated between the traditional central authority and a sincere desire to empower local communities. "MEB also came under increasing pressure from the bishops, who were caught between the movement and the state and between their own efforts to encourage lay participation while maintaining hierarchical discipline" (Mainwaring 1986, 68). That the MEB continued to exist during the military regime's rule was due to the repression of its most political aspects at the Church hierarchy's behest, and the protection of a more progressive faction of that hierarchy (46, 68). Again we see the independence of the democratic organization and its work for social transformation limited by its relationship to the central authority. And yet that central authority, the Church hierarchy, was responsible for the MEB's founding and protection at the time of the worst military repression.

The very discussion of alternative social systems was partly a result of the curriculum of the MEB, designed by its founders. Its content taught the history of capitalist development in Brazil as causing the internal dependence on international markets, the external debt crisis, the concentration of political power and money, and the exploitative relations between owner and workers. The MEB also presented the traditional Catholic Church in relation to this as influenced by capitalism: as a major landowner involved with the state and dominant classes, serving their educational needs (Wanderly 1984, 35).

In the end, the curriculum design of the MEB and the hierarchy's protection illustrate the fundamental contradiction of our model's relation to authority. A degree of independence was necessary to challenge the existing structure and yet the central authority was responsible for its founding, curbing its political activism, and protecting it from repression. This type of protection was a questionable blessing that some opted to reject; yet another instance of the agent of change choosing to represent the interests of the community rather than the central authority, and the organized community now becoming its own agency of change. An example is provided in Popular Action (AP), a main channel of radical Catholic political activity. It grew out of the Catholic University Youth (JUC), when the hierarchy tried to restrict JUC's political involvement (Mainwaring 1986, 64). AP, in order to safeguard its independence and the ability to pursue political means for social change, is another example of disassociation from the hierarchy, like CEPA in Nicaragua and the CCS in Guatemala.

Though the Catholic hierarchy did mobilize and empower the poorest of the citizenry through the MEB, Wanderly reports that a later orientation of the movement was "verification of the hierarchy" (1984, 36). In its own self-criticism and historical analysis, the hierarchy had not only organized those most marginalized in its "preferential option for the poor." For once organized and with a popular culture and ideology that spoke their self-worth, the poor developed a greater sense of independence, illustrated in a critical attitude toward the hierarchy who now felt the need to restrain their own creation. This has been verified in studies of the CEBs by Lernoux (1989), and in the particular archdiocese of Victoria, Brazil, from 1984 to the present, by Pedro Ribeiro de Oliveira of the Institute for the Study of Religion in Rio de Janeiro (1988). As the MEB development was integral to the CEB, we need to examine further the CEBs in Brazil and their relation to the MEB.

IN BRAZIL'S CHRISTIAN BASE COMMUNITIES

The CEBs grew out of the same pastoral planning of the episcopate which included the MEB. The decisive point of their emergence according to José Marins was the NBBC's Plan of Emergency, 1963–65, which included parish renovation, the cultivation of rural unions and cooperatives, and the formation of local leaders. This was preceded by courses for the episcopate, *cursillos de capaciticazion*, beginning in 1960, which emphasized the first concern of the Church as the "obligation for the liberation of the total person." Thus, in a sense, the hierarchy, the central authority, was itself trained to share its authority with the base. In three years 1,200 courses were given in all areas of the country. It was not until the elaboration of the plan of emergency by the Plan of the Pastoral Team (1965–70) that it was decided that the diverse experiences of the community organizations being formed in each parish should be called CEBs (Marins 1972, 403–5).

These plans to renovate the Church collaborated with the MEB by the multiplication of radio schools in small communities. As in El Salvador's CEBs this provided a means of coordination. The testimony of one Dutch missionary priest who established sixty CEBs in three years in his parish covering 15,000 square kilometers is not atypical. Hearing their own voices on the radio, leading their own religious services and ministering to each other increased their sense of self-worth and their rights as individuals; important requisites of our model. Being only able to pass through each community in his extended parish once or twice a year the CEBs became a structural necessity if the laity were to be reached (415).

Leaders, "*responsables,* were elected by the appropriate towns, including the *dirigente* [director] of Sunday worship without the priest" (406). Again the CEBs were first established by an external authority, or in the case of this parish in the diocese of Barra de Rio Grande, "the CEB was the result of the work of a charismatic priest" (406), the change agent. Yet as this missionary priest reported, the CEBs varied from one community to the next.

It is clear that there are great differences in the vitality of the comunidades de base from place to place. In places where the church was more present in the past, they are more alive, than in others where the presence had been scarcely symbolic. When the community is smaller it is easier to implement the comunidade de base. There are localities in which almost the total population participates including the masculine element (which still is a notable thing in this diocese). (406)

This example illustrates the importance of training, former experience, and community size for full participation in self-direction. Though verifying our model, it further qualifies it since we find that the participants' training for full egalitarian participation can be facilitated if they have had prior experience. As with our subject Don Pedro in Esteli, previous training to participation in groups such as Catholic Action or the Family of God facilitated participation in the CEB. We have seen the cursillos play a similar role in training for participation and leadership. In keeping with our model for democratic organization, the smaller the community the more viable the democratic organization.

Once established the CEB began to take on a life of its own, becoming itself the agency of change, free of the priestly or diocesan authority. With this the issue that comes to the fore is, Where does the authority reside? Does it reside in the collectivity itself as it must in a democratic organization, or in the traditional hierarchy, external to the community? As this missionary reported, "In all a church was consolidated that began to live in the absence of the priest." However, this brought with it concerns of where the organized and so empowered community would turn its efforts, "that once the movement of the comunidade de base was initiated, they were not to continue unembodied. They will be committed also to the integral promoting of the person: education, health, etc." (406). The political ramifications were not to come merely from conflict with those who previously held social and political power but in a more subtle form with the Church hierarchy itself.

Our missionary priest speaks of how the dirigente, after completing his cursillo, directed Sunday service, from the middle of the people. They received the Eucharist from each other's hands in a service "presided over by the laity," which traditionally had been executed by the priest. The ramifications for the traditional power of the clerical class and challenge to the hierarchical structure is worth this extended reference of our missionary priest.

This is how we arrived at a new ministry in the church. Who knows where it will end up? It seems we must follow this new type of presbytery. Originating in these communities, they are elected by them and in general are married. . . . It is necessary to form them without taking them out of their environment. Not in the seminaries. What level of culture will they have? . . . They would be ordained by the community in which they grew up and that elected them for a time that the community decides. . . . Who should determine who of these groups or communities should be ordained? That will be determined by the same community. (407)

However, the liberalism of this Dutch missionary was not shared by all of the Brazilian hierarchy. Though sympathetic and at first responsible for cultivating the CEBs, the hierarchy wished to keep them within the traditional Church structure and their control. This I believe is the measure of the limit of the CEBs as democratic organizations and of their independence once operating. The following is an example of the challenge to the founding authority in the religious context.

Formation of local leaders within a community's context, referred to in the above missionary's reference, is an important element to democratic organization of the CEBs and literacy campaigns. Knowledge expressed, whether religious, educational, or social scientific, in terms of their experience, is demystified and shared with the community. This removes leadership, as a reservoir of knowledge, from an elitist position—an important characteristic of our model.

In this religious context it is an important consideration with regards to the ordination of presbyters or ministers and the performance of worship service, including the consecration and distribution of the Eucharist. If the Eucharist is to be consecrated only by individuals trained and appointed from outside the group, it perpetuates an elitist class and a mystification of sacred knowledge, unavailable to the laity. As long as the ability to select members for ordination and training is done from an authority outside of the community, the democratization of the Church will be limited. Similarly with only choosing unmarried men for ordination. Our missionary priest here is pointing to the ultimate empowerment of the community where they select their own ministers for as long as they deem appropriate—an empowerment the hierarchy would not support (407).

This training of local leaders to function in the absence of the priest was a pattern repeated throughout dioceses in Brazil where CEBs were developed. Another testimony in the evaluation of the CEBs is from the diocese of Bacabal in the state of Marachao. Typically, of the nineteen priests of the diocese, seventeen were foreign missionaries, serving more than 60,000 inhabitants. For the Church to even reach those numbers it was necessary to train local leaders. For this the cursillos were an effective tool. However, the formation of CEBs, as they organized local communities, met with accusations and became embroiled in conflict. As a priest in Bacabal testified:

In our region this work is very necessary, above all because of the continued questions between owners of land and workers. . . . It is not easy to form a CEB. We have to insist always that COMUNIDAD is not equal to COMUNISMO (408).

As with the MEB, the first premise of the cursillos for the formation of the CEB was to live with the community addressed. Because of the vast distances involved in Brazil, radio programs were a tool of the cursillos as well as the MEB in training Delegates of the Word. The radio program would consist of reading and commenting on letters written by delegates and others and playing tapes of visits to various communities. This served not only to train local leaders and coordinate communities, but also developed the self-esteem necessary for our model's openness to the concerns of the participants. One establishing religious illustrated with this comment: "It is most important to tell of the enthusiasm that awakens in our campesinos, by the power of hearing their own voices on the radio, expressing their impressions" (415).

As in the cursillos in our other cases, the exercises developed group dynamics, skills of dialogue and analysis and self-esteem; all necessary for the democratic organization engaged in social transformation. In these exercises one can observe the effect that the training would have on the membership's view of authority. "In the cursillos for establishing the CEB, the dynamic intensifies interpersonal relations and breaks with authoritarianism. It establishes more authentic relations between the coordinating authority and other persons" (8). These group dynamics call for a variation of membership in those attending a cursillo so as "to represent in miniature the church problem . . . women, men, young, married, celibate, priests, religious, seminarians," and members of various church organizations (198).

The "Process of Observation" serves as an illustration. The instructions for the group read:

One of the modes of learning with regard to human comportment, is to observe what happens in a group. . . . When one observes how communications are developing, for example, who speaks, for how long, who speaks to whom. . . . Did we take into account or not who makes the decisions in each moment. . . . There can be the problem of identity—who am I in this group. . . . The problem of power, control or influence: who controls what we do, how much and what influence do I have. . . . All of the dynamic of discussion rests on the equal participation of its members. . . . Things that impede group discussion . . . to put the message at a high level above the actual capacity of the person . . . to be convinced that we are right when others consider us wrong, and to continue with our message not having conceded anything . . . the incapacity to see the point of view of another person . . . to have contempt for the beliefs, habits and customs of the other person. (48–51)

Expressed here are self-esteem, realizing the dignity of others and their opinion, demystifying knowledge by expressing it in the language and experiences of the participants, the skills of dialogue, and consensus. All of these characterize the requisites of our model. They are also essential to the success of the mass public-education campaigns, whether the MEB in Brazil or the National Literacy Campaign in Nicaragua. How then do these latter propose to be democratic organizations for social transformation and what circumstances limit their execution of the model?

PAULO FREIRE AND THE PROCESS OF CONSCIENTIZATION: ITS PART IN DEMOCRATIC ORGANIZATION FOR SOCIAL TRANSFORMATION

Similarities between the cursillos for establishing the CEBs and the method used in the literacy campaign are not coincidental. Besides their common source in the Church hierarchy and the experience of the poor, references are made in the theoretical work of each to Paulo Freire, who "was the most important of the intellectuals who stimulated new methods of popular education between 1958 and 1964 [and] is one of the most highly regarded theorists in the entire Latin American Church" (Mainwaring 1986, 68–70). Freire is not the only important theorist in popular education or the CEBs. Besides theologian José Marins, whose work we have been reviewing on the CEBs, Dom Helder Camara, the former archbishop of Recife, Brazil, was also one of the first key figures to popularize conscientization—central to the popular-education process. As an educational theorist of world renown, Freire is, however, the best known and most widely published. Looking at his process of conscientization in more detail will provide us with yet another descriptive model—further illustrations of how democratic organization for social transformation can be put into effect, in particular in literacy campaigns, and then, prescriptively, what the limitations and shortcomings are.

Freire "rejected Leninist emphasis on the need for a centralized party that makes the key decisions. [He] is committed to popular participation in the learning process and to . . . social transformation" (Mainwaring 1986, 70). Freire, believing in the dignity of all people, insists that the teacher engage in dialogue—learning from his/her students, using the everyday words of common people. He also insists that all education is political and should mobilize the poor to control their own destiny (Freire 1970, *Pedagogy;* 1973, 1985).

Freire popularized the notion of conscientization. Most simply stated, it is an awareness of how one has been historically conditioned and of the need to take action to transform one's situation (Freire 1985, 67–71). An illustration of the process of conscientization and how it promotes democratic organization is given in a two-hour long CEB exercise called "Generating Words" (Marins 1972, 99–103), fundamental to Freire's literacy process. At the direction of the facilitator, the first part of the exercise is the explanation of its objectives, which include assisting members in getting in touch with their worries and feelings, locating the items of interest to the group, and helping to establish common goals for team work. After the explanation, those attending break into smaller groups of six to eight people. During the second part, each person in the group is to write on paper a short note, "a phrase of consciousness," without signing it, in answer to the question, "How do I feel as a person? . . . as a priest . . . as a religious, married, youth, bishop, etc. . . . How do I feel living in this moment of history in this country, in this Church." Participants are instructed to write only short phrases of subject, predicate, complement; personal phrases of their lived experience, not generics. One can write up to ten phrases, using ten separate papers (100).

In the third part of the exercise, the lecture of the phrases of consciousness, the participants take turns in their groups reading one phrase at a time. During this period, nothing else is done, there are no questions for explanation, no discussion, no excuses, no comments, no hurry. At this time and if one is inspired to say a phrase that they have not yet written, they can write it and pass it to the secretary of the group. After reading each paper it is passed to the secretary. These exercises, as with the following, would cultivate the requisite openness and consensus of our model— determining the participants' concerns, insuring equal value to each expression, and the full participation of all members.

In the fourth part of the exercise, the participants begin to question reciprocally why they said one or the other thing, such as, "Was it a personal problem or one of the environment? Was it an isolated case or common in your everyday life? Something recent or of long ago?" Something that is frequent? Typical of the group you belong to—of priests, farmers, workers, etc.? Is there some indication of a solution in the short or long run? At this point no one discusses, or there is no dialogue established yet. There are only short questions and the answer should also be short (101).

In the fifth part of the exercise the generating words are identified. While the secretary of the group reads the phrases of consciousness written by the participants, the participants look for synonymous words that are "most frequently employed to indicate the state of consciousness of the group" (101).

During the sixth part of the exercise, the secretary or facilitator goes on noting the generating terms on the board. The participants elect the generating words that are "to be made more profound." They then narrow the selection to "the most generating of the generating" (102).

All the groups can study all of the selected words or two or three can be treated by each group in the seventh part of the exercise. Here they proceed "to take the juice out of the words." They make them more profound by exploring the words' existential significance, questioning: "In what context was the word spoken? When does it appear the most? What living situation is behind each of the words? What human reality is indicated by these words, what profound human problem?" (102).

Here problems in communication are discussed when persons do not speak from the "the center of their personality," "person to person," but rather as a "social image," "comporting one's self according to what is expected," or as the "function of a job." One communicates from "the center of the personality when one touches" emotions, feelings, personal memories, hopes, and life experiences (102).

In the eighth part of the exercise the secretary elaborates the summary of the discussion of the generating themes by his/her group and consults if the summary is in accord with them.

During the ninth part of the exercise the facilitator indicates the constantly recurring themes and can begin to elaborate on aspects not studied by the group, such as observations about the fruit of authentic communication: "That as persons present in common their problems they verify that many of them are problems of the group, and how therefore this can be an opportunity to find a common—how should it be—solution" (103). The facilitator can explain too that there are problems because they are not sufficiently addressed and that interpersonal communication is a result of the process of "demassification" where participants realize themselves and others as persons.[10]

The concluding part of the exercise indicates the ongoing nature of the process of conscientization. The facilitator asks the participants to reunite at another time in groups to discuss the personal and pastoral consequences of the group (103).

It may appear at first that the facilitator, the change agent, has a wide scope to move the discussion where he/she wants it to go. As I discussed in the CEB cases in Nicaragua, depending on the individual leader's style and commitment this position can be abused. However, true to our model, if the facilitator adheres to its structure, to the rules and guidelines given for the process, and to its ideology, the commitment to the value and opinion of each participant, it will be the participants who select the generating words. The accuracy of the facilitator's summation of their words must even be verified by the group, furthering the community's empowerment as the agency of change.

Although presented in its theoretical ideal form, the above reviewed exercise, "Generating Words," is one example of the local-level interaction my study of democratic organization for social transformation has sought to illustrate. We have seen other concrete expressions of this interaction in the case CEBs studied in Nicaragua, El Salvador, Guatemala, and Brazil. Freire's process of conscientization in literacy work provides another descriptive model for the exercises, for construction of democratic organization, for social analysis, and for action for social transformation coming from the group itself. Freire's process is based on the inherent dignity and ability for self-direction of the individual and group. "He believed that the goal of education should be to help people reflect on their own capacity to reflect" (Mainwaring 1986, 69).

Action, as with the CEBs, is the final trademark of the MEB. It was organized actions of the MEB participants which led to its politicization and, with the coup, its depoliticization at the behest of the hierarchy for the sake of its survival. And as we have seen, it was the desire for continued political action which led participants in the MEB, primarily university students who had served as MEB instructors, to form the politically oriented prosocialist Popular Action, free of the Church hierarchy (Mainwaring 1986, 64). This illustrates not only the inherent tension between the democratic organization engaged in social transformation and the central authority, but it also illustrates its interface with the revolutionary process. In the Brazilian case the revolutionary process, as with our others, included the call for more equitable land distribution, the socialization of health and welfare, greater taxation and control of foreign multinational corporations, the creation of political parties, and support for candidates who backed this agenda.

Political action and the resulting conflict appear to be an inevitable part of the process of forming a democratic organization for social transformation. For Freire, "'consciousness of' and 'action upon' reality are, therefore, inseparable constituents of the transforming act" (1985, 68). As with our model, for the masses to participate in the transformation of their world requires the democratic process, which in turn makes it difficult to permit them to remain illiterate. Illiteracy for Freire, and Mannheim whom he refers to, includes "the masses' lack of participating and intervening in the historical process." Rejecting a mechanistic literacy program, Freire "considered the problem of teaching adults how to read in relation to the awakening of consciousness [conscientization] . . . through acts of creation and recreation" (1973, 41, 43).

The concept of conscientization has been misinterpreted as consciousness raising, that is, simply becoming aware of one's situation. In addition, constituent of conscientization is to act on the reality one has become aware of in order to improve it. Freire elaborates that it is a matter of developing critical consciousness, that is, to represent "things and facts as they exist empirically, in their causal and circumstantial correlation" (44). Critical consciousness is contrasted with a naïve consciousness which "sees causality as a static, established fact," and magic consciousness which "simply apprehends facts and attributes to them a superior power by which it is controlled and to which it must therefore submit" (44).

It is this fatalism, characteristic of the absence of critical consciousness, which Freire confronted in his first attempt at popular education, a "cultural circle." "In the culture circles, we attempted through group debate either to clarify situations or to seek action arising from that clarification. The topics for these debates were offered us by the groups themselves." Freire describes his first literacy attempt in Recife, "with a group of five illiterates, of which two dropped out on the second or third day. The participants, who had migrated from rural areas, revealed a certain fatalism and apathy in regard to their problems" (42). Like our ideal-type model, the theoretical process of conscientization, in reality, exists rife with the limits and contradictions of the human participants and their social relations.

In the development of critical consciousness in Freire's literacy process, the first step is to study the content in which those addressed live, in order to determine their common social vocabulary. The second step is to select generating words which are chosen from confronting the social, cultural, and political reality. A group's vocabulary would then be used to teach them to read and write. The generating words would be broken down, with the root being used first to illustrate how other words are made through the combination of syllables. In the third step pictures are used to stimulate discussion, dialogue, or debate on the situation that the generating word relates to (Monteith 1977, 628–31).

Thus, illiterates are not only taught to read and write but are actively engaged in the analysis of their reality. Not only does the process require that the literacy worker live with and come to know and use the terms of those he/she wishes to instruct, but to overcome their fatalism it requires a building of self-esteem in the participants, which the dialogue and common-language usage fosters. True to our model, this egalitarian dialogue requires on the part of the educator a faith in the participants and in their dignity and ability to engage in critical self-direction. Indicating the liberation theological roots of his own thought, Freire defines this faith in his fellow humans in religious terms, referring to the theologian Karl Jaspers:

Only by virtue of faith, however, does dialogue have power and meaning: by faith in man and his possibilities, by the faith that I can only become truly myself when other men also become themselves (Freire 1973, 45).

Empathy is essential to this dialogic model of education. Dialogue therefore communicates, whereas "anti-dialogue does not communicate, but rather issues communiques" (46). It thus becomes more understandable why the long exercise in conscientization, which we have just reviewed in CEB formation, is necessary. It focuses on person-to-person communication. Speaking solely from one's socialized office, one's habitus (Bourdieu 1977), whether it be bishop to laity, or teacher to student, renders this type of authentic dialogue virtually impossible.

The major problem for the literacy program, according to Freire, is to create in the coordinators, the change agents, a new attitude of dialogue, "so absent in our own upbringing and education" (1973, 52). As with a sample CEB leader in Esteli, Nicaragua, a well-intentioned coordinator who believes he knows what is best for the participants is not engaging in listening and dialogue, nor is he/she empowering participants in their self-direction. In applying our model, this leadership style, the issue of authority within the group, is crucial in facilitating or inhibiting all four requisites of the democratic organization. If the leader does not truly represent the interests of participants, then their self-direction is limited, coordinated activities do not present their needs or methods, the equal value of each participant's opinion is not considered, and consensus is not built up. True or responsible representation, as the model suggests, would be characterized by openness—the solicitation of the concerns and opinions of all members—and dialogue as a means of achieving consensus. If this process is not adhered to then the leader or agent, no matter how well intentioned, is not "re-presenting" the group's interests, but rather his/her own.

In selecting the generative words through informal encounters with the inhabitants of the area, the coordinators are taught to select carefully words "weighted with existential meaning" and thus with "the greatest emotional content," that are typical sayings, linked to the experience of the group, and moving from less to more difficult phonetics. In the creation of generative words, of "codifications: the representation of typical existential situations of the group . . . situation-problems," are to be "decoded by the groups with the collaboration of the coordinator." Discussions lead to the development of "a more critical consciousness at the same time that they begin to learn to read and write." Though the codification represents familiar local situations, with the help of the coordinator it leads to decodification, to the analysis of local, regional, and national problems (49–51).

This illustrates not only a means of coordination, a requisite of our model, but also the demystification of knowledge and the analysis process, essential to the model's requisites of consensus and openness, so that all members can express their needs and participate fully. Thus, the community itself becomes the agency of change. No longer is the knowledge or analysis process something that only the change agent—the teacher, social scientist, politician, or priest—has access to.

An example of such a process of literacy, of decodification or demystication of the reality of the illiterate, is given by Freire in his work with cultural circles. In one such circle in the state of Rio de Janeiro, the first generative word was *favela*, slum. Freire goes on to indicate "some of the dimensions of reality which were analyzed in the discussion of those situations." In decodification of "slum," "analyzing the existential situation (a photograph showing a slum) . . . the group discusses the problems of housing, food, clothing, health, and education in a slum and . . . further perceives the slum as a problem situation" (82). At the same time the coordinator visually presents the word *favela* with its semantic links *fa-ve-la*, and its phonemic families *fa-fe-fi-fo-fu, va-ve-vi-vo-vu, la-le-li-lo-lu*. "The group then begins to create words with the various combinations." Thus they discover "the mechanism of phonemic combinations" and "the participants begin— on the same first evening—to write" (55, 83).

Freire's literacy process met with great success because it taught using the language and experience of those addressed, essential to the demystification of knowledge and the analysis process. On the fifth day of one such cultural circle, Freire reports how a previous illiterate wrote on the blackboard, "The people will solve the problems of Brazil with informed voting." Once this participant had mastered the mechanism of phonemic combinations he was able "to express himself graphically, in the way he spoke," writing "words with complex phonemes before he had even studied them" (55–56). Freire argues that achieving critical consciousness, displayed in the above created sentence, is a necessary part of educating adults if they are to teach themselves to read and write and avoid rote.

Integral to openness, the third requisite of our model of democratic organization for social transformation, is the need to recognize the worth of each individual. This includes their experience, belief system, and language. This literacy process attempts to be more natural or in keeping with the experience of those to be educated. Freire contrasts other literacy programs,

where the students must endure an abysm between their own experience and the contents offered for them to read. It requires patience indeed, after the hardships of a day's work (or a day without work) to tolerate lessons . . . talking of graces and grapes to men who never knew a Grace and never ate a grape. "Grace saw the grape." (43)

Certainly more politically neutral or complacent generating themes such as "dog" or "family" could be selected. But the purpose of the educational process, of conscientization, is to develop a critical consciousness: to examine the problems of daily life, to relate them to larger, national problems and contradictions. In a sense, the process is to draw more clearly the lines of conflict, to seek for possible solutions, and to better the lot of the most marginalized and politically powerless through collective action. This process makes no claim to neutrality.

Despite, or more likely because of its uncommon success, the National Literacy Program, which Freire coordinated, was terminated by the 1964 military overthrow of the government of President Goulart, who had supported this popular culture movement (Brown 1974, 245–56). Freire left Brazil to go into exile. His attempt to empower the masses was not to be supported by the new military dictatorship, which some, including members of the Catholic hierarchy, hailed as preventing the growth of communism in Brazil. That Freire's educational process has a political content is not debated; Freire maintains that all education is political (1985).

LIMITS AND CONTRADICTIONS

Our prescriptive model demands further questions. Does the literacy process of Freire and the MEB, or the literacy campaign in Nicaragua, or the work of the CEBs exist in a political vacuum? Who are the authorities appealed to if the traditional views of education, history, and theology are challenged? Where does the source of the new ideology that grows out of such dialogic practice lie? A purely indigenous ideology is not possible since even a traditional scholastic or a fundamentalist Pentecostal theology was at one time imported. Nor is that desirable, since the coordinator, the change agent, is to provide his/her knowledge and training as well at the service of the community's self-identified needs. Freire admits that the coordinator, the educator, or in the case of the CEBs the religious or lay leader must be trained in dialogue, listening to the participants of the group. But if no education or theology is neutral then no agent can be.

Freire also insists that themes are to be drawn from the group and the existential situation analyzed with the collaboration of the coordinator. Obviously the coordinator's ideology and background are very important to the tone of analysis which the group will then take. Even in Freire's process it would be impossible for the coordinator to be neutral. After all, he/she has the specialized skills of this educational process, this social analysis, and this historical interpretation of the background of the nation. As the specialist, his/her opinion would be highly regarded by those who have come to him/her to be educated. It seems that a measure of the reality of the dialogue—that it is not merely another indoctrination—would be the extent to which the participants challenge even the coordinator's analysis. It is crucial that the coordinator believe that the participants are capable of their own analysis of the situation and that they have tools and beliefs of how things should be with which to analyze. This is essential if authority is to reside in the group, if it is to be a self-directing agency of change—the ideological concomitant of our model's first requisite. And yet the coordinator is to provide his/her skills, knowledge, and vision at the service of the community in the analysis of reality. There is here a tension, a contradiction which exists in each of our case studies as well as theoretically in the model.

It would take a well-trained coordinator indeed to foster such unaskewed dialogue as our model of democratic organization calls for. Freire himself would admit that it is impossible for the coordinator to live up perfectly to the ideal of having "one foot in and one foot out" of the situation in which he/she is educating (Freire, interview with the author 17 July 1987). Living with the people for a short time, as in employing the best ethnographic skills, the coordinator chooses generative words and themes from their language and situation, yet they are those which his/her selective attention has chosen due to his/her background and training. Neutrality is impossible, yet the degree of interference or indoctrination by the coordinator can be minimized. This is the case if, as outlined in our model and the above sample exercises, he/she adheres to a structure which solicits the participants' concerns consensually and an ideology which advocates that the participants' knowledge and opinion must be recognized dialogically as valid as the coordinator's.

The educator, the coordinator, is trained in a particular political perspective in Freire's process and that of the MEB and CEB; one that sides with the poorest, the socially marginalized, and tries to improve their lot. Careful training is still required in dialogue, as Freire points out, so that it is a popular education, one coming from the participants' categories, concerns, and life experiences. Freire would admit that the coordinator is to side with the marginalized and to strive to provide his/her knowledge to empower them in the dialogic process to improve their lot. It is this empowerment, through community organization and its resulting acts, which threatened the traditional central authority, whether it was the Church hierarchy in the appropriation of priestly authority by the laity, or the government in land seizures.

What are the skills and tools of analysis, besides dialogue, which the coordinators bring to the task of education? If they are not politically neutral then undoubtedly they threaten the status quo by challenging the interpretation of reality, of history, provided by the traditional educational system and the politically powerful in society. If Freire's National Literacy Program had been allowed to continue and not have been terminated by the military coup,

there would have been 20,000 culture circles functioning thoughout the country. In these, we planned to investigate the themes of the Brazilian people. These themes would be analyzed by specialists and broken down into learning units . . . as we had done with the coded situations linked to the generative words. We would prepare filmstrips with these breakdowns as well as simplified texts. (Freire 1985, 55).

These themes to be investigated, Freire claims, come from the people themselves, yet the coordinator selects the ones which present "situation-problems" that "open perspectives for the analysis of regional and national problems" (1973, 51). But it is this elaboration of local problems into regional and national political debate which the coordinator's knowledge provides. And herein lies the accusation of the traditional politically powerful that this method of literacy is also indoctrination: anticapitalist and prosocialist; more likely labelled "Communist."

Freire insists that the coordinator must assist the participants to "approach reality scientifically in order to seek the dialectical connections that explain the form of reality." And this means, through dialogue and stating the existential situations as problems, employing the process of generative words, discovering "the structures that need to be transformed" (1985, 55–57). Though we might agree with Freire and the coordinators' interpretation of the problems of the poor with whom they work, it is nonetheless an interpretation, though we would insist more accurate than positing the source of the poor's plight in their work habits. When Freire lists the themes which repeatedly arose from the groups: "nationalism, profit remittances abroad, the political evolution of Brazil, development, illiteracy, the vote for illiterates, democracy," it is difficult to imagine how they could have come from "the participants, who . . . revealed a certain fatalism and apathy in regard to their problems" (1973, 42), without the coaching of the coordinator—the change agent. As in the Latin sense of the word "educate" the coordinator still is engaged in "drawing out" from the students but this elaboration of their local problems will involve the educator or coordinator's own theoretical disposition and selected tools of analysis.

A further illustration of the limitation and contradiction in this analysis of the Latin American reality is provided by the Protestant Latin American Evangelical Commission on Christian Education (*Comision Evangelica Latinoamericana de Educacion Cristiana* CELADEC), representing the traditional mainstream Protestant Churches. Presented in 1980 by the General Secretary of CELADEC to the Provincial Conference of the Episcopal Church in Panama, *Realidad Latinoamericana y Alternativa Pedagogica* (The Latin American Reality and an Alternative Pedagogy) was written to draw out the relationship between popular education and Christian education concerning "our obligation to the impoverished masses" (CELADEC 1981, 6).

The "elements of analysis" of the "Latin American reality" that CELADEC uses to "engage in its transformation" are "structural." This contrasts with Cecelia Madriz's analysis of the fundamentalist Pentecostals, who offer an individualist interpretation to the problem of poverty. CELADEC follows a sociological analysis, "that in his essence, mankind is organized in societies, *which is the only way that he has for meeting his necessities.*" The analysis goes on in classical Marxist form to examine the "contradictions" of "capitalism and imperialism," "between the bourgeois and proletarian classes," and "between imperialism and socialism" (7–13).

Without drawing out all of the analysis, it suffices for our purpose that CELADEC concludes that the work of Christian education is the work of popular education.

Here CONSCIENTIZATION is the first priority of the work of the Church, understood as a process of reflection in praxis. . . . Latin America has found in Marxism the categories of socio-political analysis required to scientifically analyze the capitalist reality of the continent. This urgency imposes on us a task of understanding a new modality of our knowing. Can one continue to be anti-marxist without being anti-revolutionary and, therefore, anti-Christian? (77)

The question then is, Does popular education, the technique of conscientization, and the construction of democratic organization for empowering the previously disenfranchised by necessity have to challenge the established central authority, the mode of production, and the traditional political apparatus? After all, this is a major cause of contradiction in our model and in the cases we have studied: Once launched by the central authority, the community, empowered in the democratic organization, challenges that authority in its bid for self-direction and social transformation. If the previous economic and political system was one in which the masses, who are now organized, had been disenfranchised, economically, politically, or socially, then this process of democratic organization will present a challenge to the pre-existing system and offer an alternative of commonly shared power. If the previous system denied the marginalized a living wage, employment, or enough land on which to feed their family, then organizing them would undoubtedly result in a challenge to the modes of production, including ownership.

In its social analysis, the democratic organization for social transformation, if it is to be independent and self-directing, must be able to apply any analysis which is available and which they choose. That may be a Marxist analysis of the ownership of the means of production and surplus extraction, or it may be a liberation theological analysis, condemning an economic system that does not provide for the needs of the most marginalized in society. They should also be able to choose a progressive developmentalist analysis or a traditional theological analysis which emphasizes individual hard work as the means of salvation and social improvement. The point is, for the first requisite of our model, independence and self-direction in relation to authorities, the participants should be able to choose whatever tools of analysis and interpretation of reality that they believe gives a more accurate understanding of their situation and which empowers them to change that through organized collective action.

Measuring the CEBs and mass-education efforts by the characteristics of a model of democratic organization for social transformation, we realize how short of the ideal these realities are. We have seen, too, the contradictions, in theory and in our case studies, between freedom from authority and the need for coordination, between openness to everyone and the need to arrive at consensus. In the end these contradictions are not resolved in practice but illustrate the complex and contradictory nature of democratic organization, and a tension which is perhaps necessary if it is to be engaged in social transformation. Another case study to help us explore this contradictory nature and the limitations placed on the ideal model by reality is the Nicaraguan mass-education campaign, the Literacy Crusade.

9

Nicaragua's Literacy Campaign

EDUCATION FOR DEMOCRATIC PARTICIPATION AND SOCIAL TRANSFORMATION

I will focus first on the Nicaraguan literacy campaign *La Cruzada Nacional de Alfabetizacion* (National Literacy Crusade, CNA), which was initiated immediately after the Triumph of 1979. Sources are unanimous about the incredible scope of the Nicaragua literacy campaign. Reducing illiteracy, from 50 percent to approximately 15 percent within a period of nine months (Arnove 1986, 19), won the campaign UNESCO's annual grand prize for literacy achievement in 1980 (Miller 1985, 13). This magnitude "meant that initially almost every person who knew how to read and write would teach those who did not . . ." (Arnove 1986, 19). There are several good sources that deal with the logistics and detail how the campaign was carried out (Miller 1985; Arnove 1986; Hirshon 1983). However, our focus is on the method of the campaign. Did it adhere to the requisites of democratic organization for social transformation as described in our model; if so how, and if not how and why did it fall short?

Immediately obvious are the contradictions of democratic organization for social transformation, particularly between the central authority's goals and the need for coordination on a national scale, and, on the other hand, the desire to be open to the participants' concerns and develop consensus in self-direction—between the models' first two and last two requisites. Ecuadoran educator Rosa Maria Torres, who worked closely on the Nicaraguan educational process, describes the literacy campaign as "a tool for the development and consolidation of the revolutionary process" (Torres 1983,

19). She refers to Paulo Freire's comments on the literacy campaign of Guinea-Bissau as equally applicable to Nicaragua's:

The fundamental question was not just to give literacy to adults nor of simply using literacy as an instrument for transforming the social reality, but with putting it (one must insist on this) at the service of national reconstruction. (Torres 1983, 22).

However, putting the campaign at the service of national reconstruction meant supporting the politics of the revolution and its vanguard party, the FSLN. The work book designed for use in the campaign, *El Amanecer del Pueblo* (The Awakening of the People) provided the generative themes to be used throughout the nation in the literacy process (Ministry of Education, MED, 1980). Each of the twenty-three lessons provided a photo for discussion, key words, and a theme sentence. The first word is "revolution," with a photo of Augusto César Sandino, the Nicaraguan guerrilla leader who expelled the U.S. Marines only to be assassinated by Somoza; the second "Fonseca," the founder of the FSLN; the third "liberation," with a photo of the FSLN (Miller 1985, 76–79).

From the content of the notebook one can see that the primer provided literacy in the context of three major thematic areas:

1. the history and development of the revolution.
2. aspects involving the defense and consolidation of the revolution, and
3. the socioeconomic programs of the Government of National Reconstruction. (Miller 1985, 76)

In short, the generative theme of the literacy campaign was the revolution which enabled the campaign to take place. However, how is this different from indoctrination by an external authority when such a campaign and its content is planned by a central authority?

Freire's literacy process calls for the local community or cultural circle to generate its own themes from the participants' experience. In this manner the content of the literacy material would be created dialogically: using the language of the community and a sociocultural analysis of that community by that community, with the help of the literacy worker's skills and knowledge (Freire 1970, *Pedagogy*; 5–80). Even the preparation of literacy materials for a Brazilian national literacy campaign was based on the dialogue and experiences of initial small cultural circles.

Some argue that in the Nicaraguan case this was impossible because of the minimal training of the *brigadistas* (literacy workers) who were mostly young people, the all-out assault on illiteracy, and the short duration of the campaign (Arnove 1986, 23). Freire himself defends the CNA's selection of the word "revolution" as "the most important word to begin the dialogue." After all was it not the revolution which enabled the CNA to take place?

His sole criticism of the choice of the word "revolution" was the "linguistic difficulties" of such a polysyllabic word at the very beginning (Paulo Freire, interview with the author 17 July 1987). However, our task is not to justify or judge the Nicaraguan literacy campaign, but to measure it against the model of democratic organization for social transformation.

First, did the authority reside in the community itself when there was not only a prepared text for the literacy work, but when it was so heavily ideological and pro-Sandinista in nature? The first training group of literacy workers, returning from their practice teaching, identified the root of the problem as a difficulty in generating discussion in lessons two and three. The images for discussion in these cases were a photograph of Sandino's face and a drawing of Fonseca. What was the problem? "Many people were not able to recognize the figures, much less have a personal identification with them." Of course we can be more sympathetic, as Miller is, knowing that "Somoza's educational system relegated the men to category of bandit and terrorist" (1985, 84–85). However, the point remains that these were obviously not themes generated by the collectivity. Authority in this case did not reside in the group but rather in an external central authority, even though that literacy commission "was composed of delegates from twenty-five public and private institutions, government ministries, universities, workers' associations, and citizens' groups" (49).

Again this illustrates a fundamental contradiction in our model and in the reality of democratic organization for social transformation; the tension that exists between independence from a central authority external to the group and the need for coordination of all groups if a common, in this case national, goal is to be achieved. To its credit, that goal, national reconstruction, was to involve communities in the decision-making process at the grass roots level and so, in conjunction with the central government, provide better social services (Arnove 1986, 40). The CNA was the first attempt to train formerly marginalized illiterates who did not even have the vote to participate in this democratic process. To voice opinion publicly, to challenge authority, when "this directly opposed ingrained traditions of subordination and self-deprecation," would not be an easy matter (25). Here the CNA does follow the model's requisites of openness and consensus—cultivating self-esteem and dialogue. This would prepare those involved for participation in other mass organizations and in their self-direction. Despite the limitations of central coordination and the prepared text, the CNA in its method tried to do this with notable success.

The method included training the brigadistas in a "pedagogy of shared responsibility." Director of the CNA, Luis Aleman, explained,

In training, we stressed popular communication, cooperative relationships, discussion, and analysis. Our aim was to help people understand that their words had value, that their ideas made sense. It wasn't us saying to them, do this or that. It was let us do this, let us build together. We wanted them to feel like artists creating a master work of great beauty. (Miller 1985, 109)

For each of the twenty-three lessons of *El Amanecer*, an introduction and discussion of the photograph contained four steps:

1. description and analysis of the photograph,
2. relation of the photograph to the learners' personal lives,
3. relation of key sentence to the photograph, and
4. examination and planning of future tasks that were implied in the photograph's theme. (83).

The dialogue was regarded by the CNA planners as a "means to reflect over the past, speak about the present, and discuss the participation of everyone in the building of a new Nicaragua" (85). As such it was a means of preparing participants for "community-action research" (93–100) and participation in mass organizations (Arnove 1986, 34–36), similar to the ideas of Colombian social scientist Octavio Fals Borda (1980).

Even though "the involvement of the entire community in research to identify, understand, and solve commonly shared problems," has been identified as "the most noteworthy innovation" in the methodology of the campaign (Miller 1985, 103), this was restricted. Because of the limits of time and training of literacy workers "the original scope of the research was reduced to a field study to be conducted principally by the volunteers themselves" (99). Again we see reality impose limits on our ideal model. Consensus, as the means of soliciting and addressing the needs of all participants based on the egalitarian belief in their self-direction, was reduced to the literacy workers themselves identifying the community's problems, albeit through living and speaking with the community.

And the limits were not only internal as with time and training but included the context of external aggression against the revolution's goals. Brigadistas were killed by contras and educators were targeted.

The aggression directed against the Sandinista regime by the U.S.–backed counter-revolutionaries is another source of problems. As of May 1984, 158 teachers had either died in combat or had been assassinated while teaching; of this number 135 were popular educators in EPB [Popular Base Education]. Educators and health workers comprise special targets of *contra* attacks as they are symbols of the social changes occurring in the country. In addition, in 1984, 840 CEPs [Popular Education Collectives] were not functioning as the result of direct sabotage or because of the danger to students attending evening classes. (Arnove 1986, 54)

Following the dialogue discussion, a ten-step teaching methodology was followed for each of the twenty-three lessons of the primer. These were selected not only to promote the themes of the revolution but to study forty-two different syllable families in the Spanish alphabet (Miller 1985, 78–79). These ten steps began with relating the lesson sentence to the previous dialogue, an explanation of the key word, its separation into syllables and the reading, tracing, and writing of the syllable family. The steps move on to the participants creating, reading, and writing their own words—a contribution of Freire's direct involvement in the CNA—and then sentences by combining the possible syllables studied. This creation of their own "words increased a learner's sense of individual worth" (Miller 1985, 91). Last of the steps, participants would write dictated words and sentences and carefully write a sentence for legibility.

As with the Brazilian MEB, the CNA participants reported an increased measure of self-worth, even from the moment of the introductory exercise when they learned to sign their own name. The very act of being able to sign one's name rather than using a thumbprint or an *X* for one's signature on documents, was noted by the previous illiterate as increasing their sense of dignity. As Don Pedro, father of my subject host family noted with pride and regret: "And I signed my name to the paper, but my friend couldn't" (Journal Entry 386, 5 September 1985). This sense of self-worth was also communicated by Rosa, Don Pedro's wife, as she would read out loud the newspaper by kerosene lamp almost every night.

An awareness of self-worth and the rights of each individual are characteristic of the ideological concomitant of openness, the third requisite of our model. It is also necessary for the fostering of critical consciousness. One must believe in the equal value of one's own opinion if one is to challenge the previous teachings, or to be critical of the socioeconomic situation and other interpretations of it, including your teacher's.

Essential to the model's requisites of openness and consensus and attesting to the dialogic nature of the CNA, perhaps its greatest accomplishment, besides literacy, was the learning done by the volunteer literacy workers, the brigadistas. Living with families, in conditions of poverty and parts of the country they had never before known, awakened in them a critical consciousness of the previous system which had maintained so many of their fellow countrymen in such oppression. Literacy workers were to keep diaries of their experiences as part of the plan of the CNA. Silvio, a brigadista, wrote, "Thus began our great work: we teaching them to sign their names and they teaching us about corn. Little by little we felt a greater coming together. We began to feel the companionship within our family" (Ocampo 1984, 73). A previous illiterate peasant farmworker spoke to a mother of a brigadista on her visit to her son:

Do you know I am not ignorant any more? I kno v how to read now. Not perfectly, you understand, but I know how. And do you know, your son isn't ignorant any more either. Now he knows how we live, what we eat, how we work and he knows the life of the mountains. Your son, ma'am, has learned to read from our book. (Miller 1982, 244)

This testifies that the dialogic process essential to the democratic organization need not necessarily result in social conflict. Such interclass dialogue can also result in social cohesion. One study which surveyed students who participated in the CNA found that literacy workers experienced a greater support for the revolutionary process, especially the middle- and upper-class brigadistas, as a result of their participation in the campaign (Arnove 1986, 30–31). As with Padre José, the Belgian missionary working with the CEBs in Esteli, the agent of change, if he/she is engaged in democratic organizing for social transformation, is also changed by the dialogic process. Julia, a middle-class brigadista, testifies to this as well as to the change wrought by participation in the CNA.

I was a snot before I went off to teach literacy. I didn't greet or talk to peasants who came into town; I fussed a lot about dressing up and making up my face, and before I put on the new boots the Crusade gave me, I filed and painted my toenails. Now that I know people from the surrounding valleys, people are always stopping by to greet me and I love it. My old worries just bore me now. (Truemann 1981)

Truemann, writing on the CNA, explained Julia's transformation.

Julia now (at the end of the campaign) knows personally how most Nicaraguans live. She spent five months eating beans and tortillas, sleeping with fleas, getting up at 4 A.M., sharing a bedroom with a whole family, hiking for miles through mud and rock without convenience of even an outhouse. She knows lots of once-illiterate people [her formerly illiterate students] whom she regards as far more talented and intelligent than herself. (297–98)

Again, however, the development of dialogue between literacy worker and illiterate was not without its difficulties and contradictions and would depend as much on the unique background and characteristics of the literacy worker as it would on the predisposition of the illiterate. Minimally trained brigadistas, many of whom were merely teenage students, could be expected to experience the prejudices of their bourgeois urban upbringing. Arnove highlights this "ambiguous and even contradictory" nature of the effect of participation in the CNA, depending on the individual's history and "changing opportunity structures within the country." He refers to Truemann's report on Julia, one year after the CNA.

Julia was a different story. She continues to volunteer for such things as health brigades and coffee harvesting, but when I asked about the revolution she wrinkled her nose, smiled and said she was "contra"—short for counter revolutionary. "She's joking," said a friend of hers, but I didn't think it was wholly a joke. And yet, when I asked her about her future, she said she wants to be an agronomist—an intriguing career choice much favored by the revolution; no other change could put her closer to the heart of the important social change. (1986, 31)

Difficulties and contradictions were also experienced in the attempt to practice the dialogic methodology of the CNA: Limits included the youthfulness and lack of training of the brigadistas and the illiterates' lack of experience of dialogue with an authority figure and the absence of belief in the value of their own opinion. Hirshon reports such a problem with Miguel, a brigadista: "I try to do it [the dialogue] right, but students say we don't want to talk politics; just get on to the syllables." Hirshon's advice to Miguel highlights the difficulty in adopting this new methodology when the brigadistas themselves were often students of traditional rote learning. "When I saw your class, you started really well, but when people remained shy, you ended up giving a speech. That's when people get the idea it's some kind of political indoctrination" (1983, 105). This indicates what might be the crucial characteristic of the change agent, the initiator of the democratic process in the community-based organization—the willingness to listen. Contradictions are evident here since the CNA's goal, cultivating support for and participation in the revolutionary process, was not of interest to some of the illiterate participants who just wanted to learn to read and write—just get on with the syllables. Part of the problem was the CNA's perhaps too rigidly predesigned lessons and goals, and the lack of the student teachers' training for dialogic education.

Admitting to these problems and contradictions, however, does not negate the CNA's accomplishments. Among these we have seen the creation of a sense of self-worth and egalitarian belief in self-direction among previous illiterate persons, a consensual means of soliciting participants' needs, and the creation of a sense of community which included the imported literacy worker. All of these are important characteristics of our model for democratic organization engaged in social transformation. We have also seen the limits to these ideals that the real human actors and historical situation provide, as well as the contradictions inherent in coordination and authority.

Those who argue that the CNA was solely a means of pro-Sandinista and prorevolutionary indoctrination fail to realize the nature of the revolution, since to be prorevolutionary, in the transformative meaning of our model, is to encourage popular participation of the masses. This participation was made possible in the CNA only because of the revolution. That the CNA was pro-Sandinista is obvious from the content of the texts. However, any attempt to cultivate democratic organization for social transformation is situated in historical circumstances which place their own limitations and demands on such attempts. In the case of the CNA, that was to consolidate the Sandinista revolution, which Freire defends as a necessary clear goal, needed if the revolution was to succeed (Paulo Freire, interview with the author, 17 July 1987). Those who argue that the CNA was too political are ignoring the politics of all education, perhaps because in their own educational system they agree with the politics and the cultural reproduction that system fosters. Most likely it is because they are the benefactors of that system which they claim is neutral; a neutrality which is impossible.

Nevertheless, this is not to dismiss the very real limits and contradictions of the CNA's attempts at democratic organization for social transformation and how this case has further qualified our theoretical model. These are even further illustrated, along with the possibilities and the successes, in *La Educacion Popular Basica* (Popular Base Education, EPB) and the mass organizations (MO) which the CNA was to encourage and be succeeded by.

POPULAR EDUCATION IN NICARAGUA

The new educational system created in Nicaragua after the Triumph is characterized by both an ideology and a structure of democratic organization for social transformation, including all of the limits, difficulties, and contradictions that go with such an organization in a nontheoretical, that is, real-life situation. From the top, the ministry of education of the revolutionary government, down to the students, a new ideology and accompanying curriculae was designed to meet the needs of Nicaragua, such as training more doctors and more agronomists (Arnove 1986).

Carlos Tunnermann Bernheim, Nicaragua's former Minister of Education, underlined the new ideology of the Sandinista approach to education in *Hacia Una Nueva Educacion en Nicaragua* (Towards a New Education in Nicaragua) (1983). He speaks of the new educational system as a means of creating a new Nicaraguan, one interested in serving the needs of his/her fellow citizen, not in self-aggrandizement.

And if the Popular Sandinista Revolution is to advocate a change of our structures in order to make Nicaragua a more just society, a more human society, egalitarian and fraternal, it is natural that the objectives of education and its philosophy must respond to those objectives, so that education can also contribute—as an important factor in that transformation—to forge in the mind of the students the conscience of a more just, more human and more fraternal society. Therefore education must effectively contribute to the redefinition, of the values of our Nicaraguan society, because we must overcome the old values that ruled us, some of the better held ones were toward an elitist and aristocratic conception of that education. (1983 16–17).

Perhaps nowhere was this ideology translated into structure more than in the EPB.

The EPB was to be heir to the CNA. Those who could not complete the literacy training in the period of the CNA were to continue their learning in *Colectivos de Educacion Popular* (Popular Education Centers, CEP), which were also to continue the literacy efforts with those who could not attend regular schooling, whether they be working youth or adults. Even before the CNA ended, the most advanced learners in the literacy program were encouraged to continue the work of teaching their peers as *coordinadores populares* (popular coordinators) as part of the *sostenimiento* (maintenance followup) to the CNA. Some of these would go on to be *educadores populares* (popular teachers) in the EPB. Most of the EPB was rural, working in small groups of approximately ten students in a CEP. The campesino nature of the program served what Torres refers to as "the strategic role that the program would play in the agricultural transformation in Nicaragua, as the axis of support for the fundamental task of the Agrarian Reform and the development and consolidation of the cooperative movement" (Torres 1982, 3–22).

As with the CNA, the EPB had a clear aim—fostering the revolutionary goals of social reconstruction. Goals which Freire argues must be established and clearly outlined if a social transformation is to take place. Regarding the texts of the EPB, Arnove notes:

The primers, for the most part, reflect not only the pedagogical notion of praxis (action guided by thought) but the political priorities and programs of the FSLN. Their content clearly is intended to safeguard and advance the Sandinista revolution as well as transform the political culture of the country. From the cover page on, the text and illustrations systematically echo the national priorities of increased production, defense, and national sovereignty. (1986, 51)

LIMITS TO POPULAR EDUCATION

The dialogic methodology of both the CNA and EPB were to prepare the previously illiterate and disenfranchised for participation in democratic organization and so their self-direction. The CEP, the popular adult educational collectives, were to prepare a rural population, previously landless or semisubsistent, for collective land ownership and the participatory cooperative enterprise that that entails. However, often having peer instructors, educadores populares, who might themselves be newly literate, had its limits.

Primary among those limitations was the stinted knowledge of the popular educators. A letter from a CEP in the department of Leon to the central direction of the EPB reads:

A revolutionary salutation: We are 7 studying and 4 already have completed El Amanecer del Pueblo and the practical exercises and we reviewed the manual, and the journal of Sostenimiento. The other three know the alphabet and can write. Now we need a teacher that can help them advance in the lessons and also in Math. With Christ and Mary we alphabetize every day. (Torres 1982, 19)

A dialogic model of education, with popular teachers who are peers of their students, may have its assets in fostering participation, but it also has its setbacks. Arnove notes:

While teacher-centered pedagogy is something that I normally do not advocate, after comparing a number of CEPs with the Ministry of Education's more traditional accelerated primary education program (CEDA), I came away with the impression that there is a lot to be said for systematic education that involves the transmission of large amounts of information in a didactic way. This [EPB] type of instruction will not contribute to another basic goal of popular education—to increase the level of knowledge and skills of people so as to further the material progress of the country (1986, 55–56).

Though his critique may be well warranted, we must keep in mind that our purpose is not so much to measure if a particular form of organization fosters material progress, but rather if it empowers by fostering participation in the self-direction of its members. In our model, material progress, including the increased storehouse of intellectual knowledge, is not the revolutionary transformation of society which is sought. It is rather full democratic participation, applied in this case to education, and in the following to other mass organizations.

10

The Mass Organizations

I will continue now to qualify the model by studying two additional instances: descriptions of its attempted application in mass organizations. It is hoped that by examining the actual meetings and functioning of a Civil Defense Committee and a farmers' association, as observed in real-life situations, I can further qualify the model; noting what circumstances cultivate its characteristics and, when it is limited, how those limitations might be minimized. First we will look at the theory and structure behind the mass organizations (MO).

The model of collective effort exemplified in the CNA and EPB was applied in the MO, as vehicles of popular participation in the social transformation, the restructuring of revolutionary Nicaragua. The model provided by the CNA was that of a multiplier or pyramid of trainers:

80 trainers (half teachers and half university students) were first prepared in a 15-day course followed by one month of field experience. These 80 then trained approximately 600. The multiplier effect then proceeded in this fashion: the 600 trained more than 11,000 . . . who trained over 100,000 literacy workers. The process took approximately three months. (Arnove 1986, 38)

In accordance with our model of democratic organization for social transformation, through the MOs the Sandinista government maintained

that when the people want a basic service they can provide it themselves through their communal efforts. The role of the government is to assist with mobilizing the population and providing material support, training, and technical advice. This approach breaks with the elitism of a model based on professionals monopolizing knowledge and exclusively controlling delivery of services in essential areas. (Arnove 1986, 38–39)

This is in accordance with our model: The demystification and sharing of knowledge is necessary for consensus and full participation so that authority might reside in the organization itself. Like the coordinator, educator, or minister applying the dialogic process to community formation, the change agent, in these cases the central authority's representative, the government specialist, such as the agronomist, is to facilitate the empowerment of the organization by providing his/her technical knowledge and resources at the service of the community. In this way the once specialized knowledge is applied by the community where it deems it appropriate and the community itself becomes the agency of change.

To continue to democratize society these organizations not only enabled the previously disenfranchised to participate in the social change, but also enabled the voluntary mobilization necessary in a poor country to meet pressing social needs. An example is the mobilization in 1981 of 70,000 trained volunteers through the *Juventud Sandinista* (Sandinista Youth, JS) and the *Comite de Defense Sandinista* (Sandinista Civil Defense Committee, CDS).[11] For three days these volunteers distributed antimalarial pills to approximately 75 percent of the population, practically eliminating malaria from a country which had long suffered from it (Arnove 1986, 38). This was accompanied by barrio cleanups of stagnant water sites that could foster malaria. These efforts won international recognition from the World Health Organization and successfully illustrate our model's need for coordination.

These mass organizations, besides the JS and CDC, also included associations for rural laborers (ATC), women (AMNLAE), unions for other than rural workers (CST), educators (ANDEN), for small landowning farmers including cooperatives (UNAG), and others. Cases of the CDC and UNAG in action should illustrate further the benefits and the contradictions of democratic organization for social transformation as exemplified in the MO.

CIVIL DEFENSE COMMITTEES

Organized by block, rural area, or village, in urban centers each fifteen to twenty CDCs formed a neighborhood committee. Above these were municipal and zonal committees that met at regional and national levels. As such the CDCs were the principal connection between the people and their government and another illustration of the possibility of coordination, requisite in our model (Serra 1982, 105–6). Like the CDC's precursor, the CEB, inhabitants of a barrio were invited to join the CDC when members went casa por casa, asking their neighbors to attend a meeting concerning the barrio's needs. In the cases I observed, these included maintaining watch of a street for certain hours of the day or armed guard at a designated post (both for detection of contra infiltration and sabotage), attempting to get electricity for the barrio, building a *casa comunal* (town hall) for meetings, addressing the problem of flooding in the rainy season, or meeting with the local representative of the FSLN over a plan of mobilization and defense in the case of an imminent contra and U.S. bombing and invasion.

Meetings were held in a dialogic format, called frequently whenever a pressing concern arose, otherwise on a weekly basis—illustrating our model's requisites of openness and consensus. Attendance was voluntary, ranging from ten to twenty, depending on the item of discussion. Those of the barrio who chose to participate could do so, or they might not attend a particular meeting because of conflicts with their schedule. Each neighborhood being just that, an area of several blocks in which neighbors knew each other, the informal lines of communication—corner-post conversation and friendly gossip—would get the word out concerning the meeting, its purpose, and decisions made. One such meeting in my subject barrio of Camilo Segundo in Esteli serves as an illustration of the empowerment of the community. A brief history of this barrio is first necessary.

A new barrio, established by squatters after the Triumph, the FSLN directorate of the town was opposed to there being a neighborhood where the inhabitants chose to squat because it was low lying and prone to flooding and because it was located at the side of the Panamerican Highway, close to Chevron and Shell gasoline stations which would endanger the barrio in case of contra sabotage of these petro depots. True to democratic character however, the barrio organized its CDC and refused to leave their sites and homes despite the FSLN's wishes. The FSLN backed down and the barrio was permitted to remain. This is an illustration of authority residing in the collectivity, however, it was successful because the central authority, the FSLN government, listened to the CDC rather than using its authority to relocate the barrio.

During the time of my field research, a barrio meeting was called by the local commander of the FSLN because the contras had recently made their major attack on the town since the Triumph. The Sandinista military feared that the attack would be backed up by bombing from U.S. planes. The meeting was well attended in a front yard of one of the neighbors, after the work day at 5:00 P.M. It was informal. Of the fifty or so teenagers, men, and women who attended, half drifted in and out of the two-hour meeting and stayed for only a part. A friend extended an invitation to join the meeting to a young woman returning home from work. The woman, smiling, answered that she didn't have time since she had to get ready for a date. Many in the crowd laughed as they returned their attention to the meeting.

Two young men received awards of recognition from the CDC leader for maintaining armed vigilance at the barrio guard post. One was fourteen. Working in a tobacco factory he was the sole male breadwinner in his family. The other, sixteen, was a student. All of this had been conducted in a jovial atmosphere with frequent jokes and interruptions from the crowd and laughter. I was surprised at the relaxed and happy exchanges when on a weekly basis young men like these were buried in the cemetery as the result of contra ambushes. Later, when I asked the leader of the CDC and father of my subject host family, Don Pedro, how they could remain happy in the face of such hardship he responded, "This war will be a prolonged war and we have to enjoy our lives too."

The commandante was introduced. He explained the military predicament, the need for preparedness and volunteers for mobilization to back up the armed forces as a second line of defense in case of a contra assault. He explained how there would be drills, signaled by the ringing of the cathedral bell. He went on to explain the need for bomb shelters in every barrio and how they should be constructed to house women and children in the case of a bombing attack. He illustrated how one northern community successfully constructed theirs. The meeting had begun with the national anthem and closed with the anthem of the FSLN. This was unusual for the regular CDC meetings, as were the size of the meeting and the chairs brought out for the FSLN commandante and his aide. Undoubtedly these were in honor of the special guests.

Of greater interest was the followup: informal discussion that began the moment the meeting broke up. Concerns were voiced by various neighbors regarding the money that would be needed, where they would get the timber for the bomb shelter construction, and how impractical that was in their barrio which flooded so easily. At the next CDC meeting the topics of discussion were as usual, the collection of money for the barrio electrification project and of building materials for the casa comunal. Months later I asked Don Pedro what happened with the idea of constructing bomb shelters. He simply commented that the people didn't want to put their work, time, money, or materials into that; what he called "preparing for death." He explained that they wished to continue with the other projects. Laughing, he added, "We want to prepare for life and light."

Also notable was the overlap in leadership and membership between the CEB and CDC, though it was not total. Indeed, during my stay a Protestant Evangelical and member of the Liberal party was elected to replace Don Pedro, who was also the barrio's CEB leader and as CDC leader. There was also overlap in meeting concerns, such as the care of war refugees, a woman who was being abused by her husband, and the casa comunal which the CDC members spoke of as a place for their town hall–style meetings and for the new children's band to practice and which the CEB spoke of as a place for their Bible study and worship services. The coordination between CEB and CDC efforts was further extended through joint ecumenical activities observed between the CEBs studied and Protestant Evangelical CEBs in Esteli.

The multiplicity of organizations also provides an illustration of openness, our model's third requisite. Though some might not join a Catholic CEB because of their different religious background, they could join a Protestant CEB or a secular organization such as the CDC or one of the various workers' organizations.

LIMITS AND CONTRADICTIONS

The contradiction between our model's first and second requisites, freedom from a central authority and the need for coordination, is illustrated in the case of the bomb shelters. When the CDC agreed with the purpose of mobilization, such as in the case of malaria prevention, they were easily mobilized. On the other hand, when such directives came from a central authority concerning the building of bomb shelters, with which the local organization did not agree, they did not participate. There was no obvious fear of the government applying pressure to build the shelters and no actions noted in the FSLN trying to apply any such pressure. Indeed Don Pedro took great pleasure in expressing that his neighborhood would not participate in the program—an indication of both their self-confidence and independence.

And yet the problem of authority seems to be essential in democratic organization for social transformation; not only in relation to the central authority and its relation to the community organization—a macro-level concern, but also internally, in the leadership of the local group—a micro-level concern. At both levels, the central authority, be that Church hierarchy, religious order, or the state, and the group leader, coordinator, or educator, must be committed to the dialogic methodology and the egalitarian ideology if there is to be full participation of the membership in self-direction. At both levels the agents of change, providing a link between the macro- and micro-levels, must be committed to empowering the local community, making it the agency of change, by representing its concerns to the central authority more than promoting the central authority's or their own concerns.

At the micro-level, psychologically this involves cultivating new attitudes within leaders and participants. We have seen such attempts in the cursillos of the CEB and MEB, but such change is not easy.

As the leaders of the FSLN noted on many occasions, the 19th of July 1979, was only *one* victorious battle in the ongoing war for the liberation of the Nicaraguan people. How could the enormous weight of behavior, attitudes, and values nourished by the old social system be thrown off overnight? How could corruption, alcoholism, apathy, egoism, individual lust for power and riches, *machismo*, violence, and authoritarianism be eradicated? If the experience of other countries in transition to socialism teaches anything, it is that old ideological legacies have much more weight than revolutionary theory supposes. (Serra 1982, 102)

This is not to say that the attempt at revolutionary transformation is merely one of ideology or attitude. Even with the changes in structure of organizations after the revolution, if not accompanied by a change in ideology and in the attitude of participants these organizations are still open to similar abuses. This has been described as the abuse of power or "errors committed by some novice or opportunistic leaders" (Serra 1982, 103).

We have seen cases of this; with the well-intentioned literacy worker who lacks the patience, training, and belief in the illiterate campesino needed to cultivate authentic dialogue. And we saw it in the case of the overly enthusiastic CEB leader who dictates situations and concerns to the group rather than soliciting them from the group. Another illustration is provided by my host family in Managua where I spent extended stays over a three-month period during my research in libraries and archives in the capital.

Well educated and middle class, both husband, Fernando, and wife, Isabela, had completed high school and had some years of college education before the Triumph. He had a quality control job in a cooking-oil factory, and she was raising three young children and supplementing their income as a seamstress at home. Living in a middle-class neighborhood, conditions for them had worsened since the Triumph. They complained of the scarcity of things in the market and that their salaries no longer bought as much. Though he had an uncle in the Sandinista armed forces and had lost his father in the insurrectional fighting, Fernando was resentful of the Sandinistas and openly expressed this resentment.

When pressed as to why he was so resentful and would not join the CDC or any of the Sandinista MOs, he recounted the following story.

My daughter and her young friend were sitting on the steps above the curb one afternoon in front of the house. A car came swerving down the street, jumped the curb and hit my daughter and her friend. [He gently pulls his daughter over and shows the large scar on the side of her leg.] The man driving the car was Sandinista military, in uniform. He was drunk. When the Sandinista police came they let him go without doing anything to him. And why? Because he was Sandinista. (Journal Entry 1101, 14 December 1985)

Such nepotistic abuses are not unique to any system, but they threaten all the more the morale and credibility of a system which purports to have structured itself in such a way as to avoid such abuses. However, that Fernando was able to vent openly his frustrations over this abuse of authority without apparent fear indicates that he did not expect this in the new revolutionary society. It also indicates that he did not fear reprisal from the Sandinista authorities for refusing to participate in their endorsed organizations and for being openly critical of the government, something which was hard to imagine under the Anastasio Somoza regime.

Such an abuse by the Sandinista central authority indicates the limitations of structure in creating democratic organizations for social transformation. Participants and leaders must adhere to a concurrent ideology, as our model indicates, if they are to use the structure as it was intended: in the defense of the individual's egalitarian rights. The limitation in such an instance remains the limitation of human nature: the desire for power and willingness to abuse the authority of one's office in self-interest. This abuse occurs even when one believes that in one's enlightened self-interest one is acting for the good of the organization or community. To change this a dialogic structure and an ideology of service are important, but as with any changes in character, personality, and attitude they require long-term commitment and constant watchfulness and suffer from the limitations of the real human beings who participate in it. Yet the dialogic structure and ideology of openness and consensus, characteristics of our model, enable humans to participate more fully in ongoing social transformation.

THE FARMERS' ASSOCIATION

The case of two *Union Nacional de Agricultores y Ganaderos* (UNAG) meetings serves as yet another illustration of democratic organization for social transformation in effect. Attempting to operate in real-life situations—with the restrictions of a particular context and human actors—again illustrates the limits certain circumstances place on our model, as well as their benefits and difficulties for democratic organization engaged in social transformation. UNAG, the Sandinista-affiliated association for small and medium landowning farmers, includes cooperative owners. UNAG has been described as raising the "participatory levels of peasant farmers" (Arnove 1986, 31).

I attended a meeting of the head of households of a cooperative on the outskirts of Esteli. Besides a representative from the local UNAG office, a FSLN military representative was also present because of the contra attacks which had killed a cooperative member two weeks prior. Some dozen families own this cooperative which produces *granos basicos*, corn and beans. Most were landless before the Triumph, some had semisubsistent landholdings, too small to feed their families and themselves, and so they joined their land to the cooperative. Joining a cooperative facilitated the acquisition of state-guaranteed loans in the years after the Triumph (Collins 1986).

At the meeting I attended, the rotation of duties was discussed. Who was doing what? Was everyone doing an equal share of the work? Throughout, the atmosphere was relaxed, frequently interrupted with jokes and laughter, though it was a structured meeting with the cooperative's secretary, treasurer, and chairperson of the meeting sitting at the front, with the UNAG and FSLN representatives off to the side waiting their introductions to speak. After the division of work was discussed among the membership with the assistance of the secretary, the UNAG representative was introduced and led the discussion of the productivity of the cooperative. Though in the UNAG office in Esteli a chart of projected quotas for each area was on the wall, there was no mention of quotas at the meeting. The production of the cooperative was merely stated by the secretary with comments from those attending concerning the drought and contra attacks which were limiting what they hoped to produce. The secretary also read how much of the produce went to each family according to its work productivity and how much was needed by each family to feed itself. This was interspersed by jokes from the members on the size and appetites of the various families.

The treasurer went on to discuss the financial state of the cooperative, how much was owned in government-guaranteed bank loans by each family, how much a family's debt had increased or decreased. Again there were jokes which were always thrown out by those in attendance and never taken badly. In this instance, one campesino commented on another's increased debt, saying it was due to a new saddle which he had purchased. There was laughter and a return of attention to the treasurer who was reading out the accounts. After the accounts were read the government's UNAG representative gave a short talk on the necessity to maximize production so as to pay back government loans. Questions came from those in attendance concerning what the price of their products would be since the harvest was poorer than usual. The UNAG representative said that that would be discussed at a regional meeting in Esteli (described below) of all UNAG members and other nonunion landholders who had also been encouraged to attend. Before closing, the FSLN representative spoke on the necessity to maintain vigilance for contra attacks, explaining what the military was doing and what the latest contra activities in the area had been.

At the regional UNAG meeting, held in an Esteli school classroom that was packed to overflowing with more than seventy men, the government's UNAG and ENABAS representatives presided. Again a Sandinista military representative was also present. ENABAS *(Empresa Nacional de Alimentos Basicos)* is the government organization responsible for the purchase, export, and distribution of basic foods. Those in attendance, representatives of cooperatives and local campesinos who had private holdings, were dressed in their Sunday best. For some more distant from the town, this was their major trip to Esteli, perhaps for months. Some of the private landholders were not even members of UNAG. After the meeting, in asking one such nonmember campesino why he still attended the meeting, he said it was because he had been invited by the UNAG representative who still helped out small producers such as himself with loans, seeds, and technical assistance. Then sullenly he added, "And because the guardia had tortured me," implying his reason for supporting the revolution.

The main subject of discussion was the price to be set for the corn and bean harvest. The UNAG representative explained the regional and national production for the season, while the ENABAS representative spoke of the need at basic grain distribution centers. These centers provide corn and beans at the lowest prices available to expendios—such as the one run by my subject host family—so that the poorest families were guaranteed the essentials. After this a lively discussion ensued, almost heated at times, concerning how much more money could be made by selling to private merchants who sold at the public marketplace. Upon this comment another campesino interjected, "Don't you remember before the Triumph, when you sold to that same merchant when we had a surplus production and he would give you almost nothing and so you became indebted to him with loans." A hot debate followed with various campesinos jumping in, some explaining the need to have higher prices if they were to pay off their own debts to the government, others saying that the government never demanded repayment of loans as the private merchants had. Though the debate involved shouting, standing up from seats, and some visibly upset red faces, there was still laughter and joking by others throughout which tempered the meeting.

Through the course of the dialogue, high and low prices were written on the board: what they would be paid for selling their crops to ENABAS and what would be the resulting necessary charge at the government expendios. After more than two hours of discussion, including the pros and cons of marketing through ENABAS, the benefits of working with UNAG—including the fact, as one campesino put it, that some used little of the UNAG assistance and that they could get a higher price on the private market—a consensus was arrived at with a fixed price for the sale of corn and beans to ENABAS. However, as the UNAG representative and individual campesinos had made clear throughout the meeting, it was understood that each would sell to ENABAS in accordance with the assistance they had received from UNAG in conjunction with MIDINDRA (Ministry of Agricultural Development and Agrarian Reform Institute) and MICOIN (Ministry of Internal Commerce) and, it was implied, how much they wanted to assist the revolutionary process. The comments of the individual campesinos also made it clear that above the amount which each was to determine to sell to ENABAS, everyone knew that they kept their best beans and corn to sell on the private market for the best prices. There was some laughter as campesinos would name other campesinos who did this.

At the end of the meeting the Sandinista military representative spoke of the recent contra activities and movements and encouraged the constant armed vigilance of the campesinos; to take turns watching for contra movements and to be alert to the possibility of attack. Several questions concerning their protection from the contras were asked by those attending. As the meeting ended I asked the private landholder, with whom I had spoken earlier, if he would sell his harvest to ENABAS. He explained that he would sell most of it to them because he wanted to support the revolution (Journal Entry 281, 25 August 1985).

However, government figures show that this "most" sold to ENABAS was only 14 percent when the government aimed for 40 percent so that it could prevent speculation and accompanying inflation, and set a price for the basic foods which would be affordable for the poor. As it was, the government would have to import to provide ENABAS with its 40 percent control of the market (Collins 1986, 119–39).

This Sandinista form of cooperative persuasion and dialogue, positive rather than punitive, is indicative of the contradictory nature of our model—freedom from the central authority and yet the need to coordinate and cooperate with the central authority if the revolution is to succeed. It was also costly to the Sandinista government. The benefit was support for the FSLN and the revolutionary process. The cost was a great one financially. The inability or unwillingness to apply greater pressure for the repayment of loans and increased production added to the government's indebtedness (Collins 1986, 106). This meeting also illustrates the tension inherent between coordination through a central authority and consensus as a decision-making process, as well as the pressure brought to bear on the dialogic process by the larger social context: outside forces, the contra war, drought, market prices, and world economic forces.

11

Conclusion

The problem that this study has addressed is how to cultivate local-level organizations, based on participatory democracy, which empower members to oppose an oppressive authority and participate in a revolutionary reconstruction of society. The method employed in addressing this problem has been qualitative, historical, and comparative. Moving between data on organizations which purport to be democratic and engaged in social transformation—that is, empowering the previously disenfranchised and marginalized—and theories of democratic organization and revolution, a theoretical model was constructed. This ideal type presented four necessary and sufficient requisites for a democratic organization engaged in social transformation. Our descriptive models indicated the need of a change agent which or who mediates these characteristics.

Each of these requisites have ideological characteristics concomitant with their structural aspects and include:

1. independence from the central and external authorities, and the right to self-determination with authority residing in the collectivity;

2. a means of coordinating the local-level organizations with other organizations and with the central authority, and a recognition of their interdependence and the need for coordination to achieve common goals;

3. an openness of membership, opportunity for meeting, and of expression of the concerns of members, and the recognition of the worth of each individual, their opinion and their rights; and

4. a consensual means of soliciting and addressing members' needs, and an egalitarian belief in the full participation of members.

A theoretical model, an ideal type, however, is not reality. It does not demonstrate the complexity of what constitutes a popular Church, the Pentecostal movement, the evolving nature of the traditional Church and the educational process. Nor does a theoretical model tell us how its requisites might be executed. In studying the Nicaraguan CEBs as our primary case study, and in the other comparative cases of CEBs, educational campaigns, civil defense committee, and farmers' association, I moved from a theoretical model to a descriptive model, so as to promote the dialectic between theory and data. The descriptive model illustrates how the ideal type is executed in a concrete situation, such as the CEBs participating in the revolutionary transformation of Nicaragua. And while the descriptive model illustrated how the theoretical model is approximated by what the CEBs in Nicaragua attempted to do, more importantly, articulating local-level interaction enables us to qualify the ideal type; indicating contradictions and limitations both within the case studied and in the theoretical model.

This dialectic between theory and data, between theoretical and descriptive models, suggests possible solutions to the problem of cultivating democratic organization for social transformation. Foremost among the contradictions has been the model's first requisite: the organizations' relation to the central and external authorities. This contradiction also raises the problem of the relationship between macro- and micro-levels of analysis and the role of the change agent as a link between the community-based organization and the central authority.

In North American community development studies, this situation of the change agent has been presented as a dilemma of roles; whether to represent vertical ties (to the external or central authority) or horizontal ties to the community (Warren 1963; Christenson 1980). The change agent, be that an individual or the community-based organization itself, must often make the difficult choice of siding with the community and against powerful authorities who control resources (Alinsky 1946, 1971).

The democratic organization does not exist in isolation but within a context: social, political, and economic. I have focused on the micro-level analysis. To complement this, we need to study how macro-level structural concerns of power and conflict, of the state, and political and economic constraints articulate with the micro-level. By studying how individuals are empowered in the organization, I have suggested that the organization plays an intermediary role between micro- and macro-levels, in particular with regard to social change. The coordination of local level organization to affect social transformation again involves the macro-level. This need for coordination suggests that the democratic organization must build bonds that link its membership with like-minded reformers. Thus they can present a united front, necessary if they are to succeed in opposition to a central authority who wields power over them.

Though it need not always be so, in examining our particular cases the intermediary representing the central authority in its relationship to the organization, and in coordinating organizations, regularly came to be a person, or persons—the agent of change. This change agent is an important mediation or link between the micro- and macro-levels. In each of our cases, democratic organization did not spring spontaneously from the community but was initiated by an agent. That agent, missionary or local religious, trained Delegate of the Word, literacy worker or brigadista, or representative of the Ministry of Agriculture and Agrarian Reform, is a representative of the external, central authority. As such, that agent not only illustrates the contradictory nature of the organization's relationship to external authorities, but also provides a link between the local micro-level interaction, the community-based organization, and the macro-level central authority, be that Church hierarchy, a missionary's religious order's headquarters, the state's Ministry of Education or Agriculture, or even the coordinating body of the mass organizations themselves, regionally and nationally.

When that agency of change is the community itself, natural differentiation inevitably resulted in the selection of local leaders as the principal agents mediating between the community and the central and external authorities.

In most cases the agent, the initiator of the democratic organization for social transformation, was also a representative of a central authority. However, our theoretical model requires self-direction by the full participation of the membership. A contradiction results because of the relationship with the central authority who, through the agent, has founded the community-based organization, and seeks to maintain control of it. If the organization of the community empowers it to engage in social transformation, and in that democratically self-directing, then inevitably it will come in conflict with the central authority which seeks to control its offspring's direction. This was the case with the Church hierarchy and the CEBs in each of our national studies. This was the case with the initiators of the educational campaigns, Brazilian hierarchy or Sandinista government and the collectives of learners, and between the Sandinista government and the CDC and the farmer's cooperative. Does the democratic organization empower participants to ongoing self-direction, engaging them in social transformation, or are they constricted by the macro-social context within which they are situated, including the concerns of the central authority?

That social context is limiting because it is not democratic. It is a hierarchical Church, a repressive military dictatorship, or a centralized government plan. The effectiveness of the model for empowering is limited by the ability of the agent to implement the model, to mediate between macro-level constraints and micro-level conditions. In noting these limits and contradictions in each case studied, though not explicitly, a third, a prescriptive, model was created; a result of the dialectic between data and theory, between descriptive model and theoretical model. Noting the limits and contradictions of our theoretical and descriptive models, indicating circumstances under which the requisites of democratic organization for social transformation are not met, I pointed out in the prescriptive model how the agent does not adhere to the structural and ideological requisites of our theoretical model and suggested how he or she might, based on the successes of other descriptive models.

Moving between data and theory, between descriptive and theoretical models, I will continue here to elaborate on the prescriptive model—suggesting what could be done to counter the limits and resolve the contradictions. I will continue the focus on the agent and the micro-level, but we must first address the agent's relation as an intermediary to the macro-level, central and external authority.

Being a representative of the central authority, the agent is immediately limited by the interest of that authority. "The preferential option for the poor" was after all an option made for the poor, not by the poor, but by the theologians and religious. The CEBs were started by the hierarchy and religious orders in order to reach those whom the Church could not reach. As such the CEBs were a structural necessity if the Church was to extend its influence. However, once formed and actively engaged in self-direction and social transformation, the CEBs challenged the existing power structure of the state, often representing the landholding class, in such matters as land claims. Traditionally legitimating the state and directing the laity, the hierarchy found itself in the position of trying to limit the democracy and self-direction of the CEBs.

In relation to this macro-level pressure, from Church hierarchy and state apparatus, the agent could either side with the central and external authorities and attempt to curb the CEBs, or could throw his/her lot in with the CEBs—to use whatever influence he/she had to protect and further their case with the central authority. The latter we have seen in the case of Padre José, the Belgian missionary in Esteli, who refused to close his church doors, giving the keys to his parishioners and claiming, "If I am recalled by my superior, I will not go. I am here to serve the people and they will determine whether I stay or go." This also was the case of Archbishop Oscar Romero who was assassinated for his decision. Others, however, have buckled under the pressure of the central authority. The bishop of Esteli, at the direction of the cardinal, withdrew support from the CEBs he had initiated. Maryknoll missionaries were expelled and Jesuits withdrew from Guatemala in the face of persecution to the point of assassination.

Indeed this macro-level context, in which the agent must choose to side with the community-based organization or central authority is usually beyond his/her control. Even the progressive Archbishop Paulo Averisto Arns of São Paulo, defender of the CEBs, suffered from the directives of a reactionary central authority as the Vatican divided his archdiocese, the largest in Brazil, into five, reducing his authority to only one portion (Tyson 1989, 193). Similarly, Dom Helder Camara, famous for promoting conscientization, has reached the mandatory retirement age, and his successor in the archdiocese of Recife, appointed by the Vatican, has dismantled most of Dom Helder's programs and work with the poor, three decades of organization, and prohibited him from speaking to the public (Lernoux 1989, 6).

The agent's ability to represent the interests of the community-based organization depends structurally and ideologically on his/her independence from the central external authority and how much support he/she has from the community-based organization. Is it sufficient support for the representative, the agent, to challenge a traditionally hierarchical structure and ideology? Undoubtedly the attempt at democratic organization for social transformation is more successful when supported by the central authority, as with the CNA in Nicaragua, and the CEBs in El Salvador during Romero, and in Brazil before the Vatican's challenges to liberation theology tempered even the most progressive bishops (Tyson 1989, 194).

But the support of the central authority for the democratic organization for social transformation can be a mixed blessing when that support is motivated by a desire to control the outcome, as we have seen with the pro-Sandinista content of the CNA. How well the CEBs are able to continue functioning depends on their belief in their self-direction and the absence of repression—their ability to criticize even their founders.

However, the agent does have greater control over the micro-level aspects of his/her choice to represent the interests of the central authority or that of the community-based organization. Fundamental to this aspect is the agent's training and ability to listen, in a dialogic manner, to the concerns of the organization. Also important here is the agent's commitment to an ideology which promotes the self-direction of the group and values the participants' opinions in this self-direction. As noted earlier, if the agent is not so committed, his/her zeal to improve the lot of the disenfranchised may create a means of indoctrination of the organization.

There are ways in which the agent can maximize his/her representation of the community in organizing it. In the ideal of the CEBs and literacy campaigns, the organizing agent is first to live and practice with the community, so that the community's language may be used, their concerns and experiences known. This was more strictly executed in the descriptive model of the literacy work of Paulo Freire, in the conscientization of the cultural circles. It was done to a lesser extent in the CNA, where time and a national agenda—support for the revolution—dictated the content of much of the lessons. Once having intervened on the side of the powerless (Laue and Cormick 1978, 217–18), the agent must minimize his direction by leaving control in the hands of the indigenous leaders (Robinson 1980, 88). We have seen this in the sage advice of the missionary Smutko in his work in Nicaragua.

Employing this methodology of dialogue with participants—listening to their concerns, utilizing any tools of analysis, whether Marxist social analysis or liberation theological analysis—becomes just another tool to assist the community in its self-direction. Not adhering to such an open and consensual model—proposing only one exclusive approach, employing any ideology—can become a means of indoctrination at the hands of the change agent. The CEB exercise of "Classes," representing various positions, provides an example of how dialogue can be kept open to include even disparate approaches. Conflict is not inevitable, but rather, reconciliation, compromise, and consensus are the goals.

In contrast we have seen how central and external authorities can and have abused their power by using culturally sensitive ideological labels, in particular "Communist" and "tools of the devil," to brand and discredit these attempts at participatory democracy. Indeed the CEBs and these attacks on them illustrate that religious ideology is a valuable cultural resource (Beckford 1989). The CEBs demonstrate how religion is a resource that can be mobilized, not only because of its ideology—though it is crucial for legitimation of action—but also because of the concomitant patterns of interaction. These social structures and accompanying ideologies together socialize participants to their part in shaping and being shaped by the society in which they live. Their training of members in democratic participation and the crossing over of membership to other politically active groups guarantee that, despite the uncertainty of their structural future, this will not be the last word on the impact of the CEBs.

The prescriptive model presented exhorts the organization's participants to believe in the value of their opinion, their rights, and the right to self-direction. This is undoubtedly difficult without prior experience of participation in self-direction and with a traditional ideology which fosters obedience to the central authorities. I recall the testimony of one CEB participant in Nicaragua, "The bishops are our leaders, we cannot do without them, but right now they are not listening." A new religious discourse is evolving in the CEBs, and must succeed if democratic organization for social transformation is to thrive within them.

This discourse recognizes the fallacy of a dualism which posits religion as outside of the realm of politics, believes in the equal value of the opinions of lay believer and bishop, and demands that the hierarchy listen to and serve the needs of the laity. It is evidenced in the criticism of a religious authority who does not support the democratic organization for social transformation, such as with Maria in Esteli, criticizing the parish priest who had supported the CEBs, but with the cardinal's directives, turned against them because of concern for his own security. However, for such belief in self-direction, not only is an ideology of self-worth required, but to cultivate that, a structure must supply the training for participation in the skills of analysis, dialogue, and consensus. Thus created, once set in motion, the community-based organization sets off on its own course. A valuable cultural resource indeed, it challenges the traditional institutions to a democratic participation.

In coordinating the community's efforts with others who seek a common goal, a structure must provide a means by which each group's interests can be represented and consensually integrated into common actions. In such a linkage from the micro-level to macro-level transformation, the agent must re-present the interests of the local organization to the central authority and not be merely a mouthpiece, disseminating the decrees of an elite political party or the central authority. This is the ideal behind the CEBs, the educational campaigns studied, and Nicaragua's mass organizations. The extent to which these descriptive models continue to serve as democratic organizations engaged in social transformation is predicated on the extent to which each agent acts as a representative of the interests of its members, and not the interests of a central, external authority, nor even in one's own enlightened self-interest of what one believes is best for the organization.

Because of the macro-level restrictions—the power, control, or force which the central and external authorities may be able to exert—the local democratic organization for social change is most successful where it is supported by what is perceived as a legitimate central authority. The central authority must allow the organization to function in a self-directing manner. The absence of intervention by external authorities also fosters the organization's success. However, because of these restrictions, it is necessary that the organization seek protective allies within those authorities, or maintain or assume an independence from those authorities. The latter was the case with CEPA in Nicaragua, the United Popular Action Front in El Salvador, the CCS in Guatemala, and AP in Brazil. The other alternative is for the democratic organization to be subsumed within the central authority which then comes to use the organization for its own interests. This of course is not self-directing or engaging in social transformation. However, it is a very real possibility for the future of the CEBs, because they are reluctant to disassociate from the central authority, a Church hierarchy, which, because of conservative appointments from the Vatican, continues to curtail CEB activity (Tyson 1989).

That the theoretical model is not encountered in its ideal type form in the descriptive models studied is not a surprise. It is the purpose of an ideal type to draw up the characteristics that are necessary if a descriptive model is to approximate it; in this case as a democratic organization for social transformation. The theoretical model provides us with a measure of democratic organization engaged in social transformation, the ideal type used to measure the descriptive models of our case studies. The descriptive models of the CEBs, educational campaigns, and other mass organizations have provided illustrations of how the requisites of our theoretical model have and can be executed, as well as how they can be inhibited. The prescriptive model has provided suggestions of how the descriptive models might reinforce certain characteristics of the theoretical model which circumstances of the various cases limit.

From the descriptive models we have been able to study the dynamics of local-level interaction and illustrate ways in which community-based organizations can be built—going door to door, using common concerns or traditions and existing institutions as means of creating community. They have also indicated the need for training in and possible exercises for cultivating self-esteem and skills of dialogue, consensus, and social analysis. Further detailed study of local-level interaction of democratic organizations engaged in social transformation can only further qualify our theoretical model and enrich our study; providing suggestions for its application to First and Second World countries.

Though much can be learned from the Latin American experience, applications could also be modified to different contexts. With North American communities often not spatially but more network oriented (Kadushin 1966; Crump 1977; Walker 1977; Wellman and Leighton 1988), new and innovative means of engaging individuals of limited liability (Janowitz 1952) must be devised. Though "door to door" may work in some communities, focusing on centers of congregation, such as shopping malls, churches, the workplace, and the use of mailings and electronic communication are possible means of linkage in order to involve the diffuse population of industrialized societies.

Undoubtedly more detailed analysis of how democratic organization is executed in descriptive models would assist the development of prescriptive models in the analysis and criticism of existing institutions that purport to be democratic and empowering. The theoretical model generated by this research provides a measure and the cases studied have indicated that central and external authorities have more often than not abused their power by painting as the specters of communism what in fact are the roots of democracy.

Notes

Throughout emphasis is that of the author cited.

1. Weber develops his theory of domination inherent in bureaucracies, even in democratic society.

2. Marx's classic "The Eighteenth Brumaire of Napoleon Bonaparte" illustrates how revolutions—led by the middle class or bourgeois, using the masses for overthrow—once accomplished, are usurped by the bourgeois for their self interests.

3. By grass roots organization we mean coming from and involving the most basic unit of that organization. In the case of the Church, that is the laity. My study attempts to focus on this unit of analysis, whereas traditionally, most studies of the Church in Latin America have focused on the more easily accessible hierarchy.

Although I use the term "Christian Base Community" or "CEB" throughout, in Nicaragua the term did not come into popular use until after the revolutionary Triumph. Before it was just called "community" or "Church community."

4. The worker priest is a European reform movement of the twentieth-century Catholic Church. Catholic priests became employed in occupations of their parishioners so as to bridge the social class distance between clergy and laity.

5. Just as the CEBs vary, some being traditional and devotional, so do the cursillos. In Brazil, there is some concern that traditional cursillos are being encouraged as an alternative to the CEBs (Comblin 1983).

6. "The English term consciousness-raising is not normally associated with the development of political awareness and has a more individualist orientation than does the Spanish term concientizacion. The latter term implies group process and political action, so we use it throughout, translating it as conscientization" (Dodson and Montgomery 1982, 179).

Whereas in English two separate words, conscious and conscience, respectively signify awareness and moral obligation, in the Latin languages there is but one word signifying both, such as the Spanish *conciencia*. Therefore, conscientization, from the Spanish *concientizacion*, signifies not only a greater awareness of how things are, that is, consciousness-raising, but also a greater sense of how things ought to be and one's moral obligation to act in that matter.

7. The debate between monists, who see all aspects as parts of the whole, and dualists, who claim to capture the essence of a subject in one aspect of it, also exists in the social sciences. This is discussed at length by Leaf (1979). Of course those who argue that revolution can be reduced to ideology motivating the individual actors are equally reductionistic.

8. Again, it is necessary to point out that this is an oversimplification for analysis by our ideal type model. As with all of the national episcopal hierarchies, the Guatemalan Church is a complex bureaucratic institution, with an internal dynamic constituted by multiple tendencies that have evolved and been refined over time. Actual statements by the Guatemalan hierarchy, going back to the 1930s, show that some members were conservatives, not all. The Guatemalan bishops have not monolithically supported the Guatemalan government. Prelates such as Gerardi and Mario Rios Montt are notable critics of the government. Particularly in the last ten to twelve years, bishops such as Archbishop Prospero Penados of Guatemala City, have been among the government's harshest detractors (Handy 1984, 270; Chicago Religious Task Force on Central America 1987, 43). Similarly, scholastic theology has a rich and dynamic history with various tendencies.

9. Not all Protestant Evangelical congregations were so reactionary and conservative however. Protestant CEBs also existed and Protestant pastors were included amongst those killed for their organizing activity (Greenhalgh and Gruenke 1982).

10. Massification has been the result of requiring humans to behave mechanically, such as in the technology of mass production, though technology is not necessarily massifying. "By separating his activity from the total project, requiring no total critical attitude toward production it dehumanizes him." With constricted horizons the human is made into "a passive, fearful, naïve being" (Freire 1973, 34).

11. See Chapter 4 for the origin of the CDC in the CEB. At the time of my field research in 1985, I heard the CDC, the *Comite de Defensa Civil*, also referred to as the *Comite de Defensa Sandinista* (Sandinista Defense Committee). A debate ensued in the CDS nationally and in each barrio: a self-critique about the CDS's shortcomings. Although this debate may seem symbolic it is indicative of a fundamental contradiction in democratic organization between the independence of organizations and the relation to a central authority—between the CDC and the Sandinista government. In this process of self-evaluation it was decided by some barrios to change the official name of the organization to CDC, which it had been referred to by some before the Triumph. The reason given was that they felt that the name CDS too closely associated it with the Sandinista political party when membership was open to everyone—characteristic of our model's requisite openness. In the barrio of my subject family in Esteli this was the case, where shortly after the self-evaluation, the newly elected leader of the CDC was a member of the Liberal political party. He had been a participant previously, when it was called the CDS.

Glossary of Acronyms and Foreign Language Usage

Throughout the text, translations from Spanish and Portuguese are my own unless otherwise noted. Words set in *italics* are defined elsewhere in the Glossary.

AMNLAE Asociación de Mujeres Nicaragüenses "Luisa Amanda Espinoza," the Sandinista women's union, "Luisa Amanda Espinoza" Association of Nicaraguan women

ANDEAN Nicaraguan Educators' Association, the *Sandinista* teachers' union

AP Popular Action—a political party of radical Catholics encouraging popular local power in Brazil

ATC Asociacion Trabajadores del Campo, Association of Rural Workers, the *Sandinista* farmworkers union

Barrio Neighborhood

El Bloque The Block, the name given to the regional organization of *CEBs* in northwestern Nicaragua

Brigadista *Sandinista* name for a volunteer educator in the national literacy campaign

Campesino Latin American term for peasant farmer

Casa Comunal Town hall

Casa por casa (Casa em casa) Door to door

Catholic Action Pre-*Vatican II* popular movement in the Catholic Church, which encouraged parish organization to improve conditions of the laity and offer an alternative to Marxist and Communist organizations

CCS Los Cursillos de Capacitacion Social, Seminars for Social Empowering—similar to the *cursillos*

CDC Comite de Defensa Civil, Civil Defense Committee—the local neighborhood militia in post-*Triumph* Nicaragua

CDS Comite de Defensa Sandinista, *Sandinista* Defense Committee—often used interchangeably with *CDC* in the decade following the *Triumph*

CEB Comunidade Eclesia de Base, Christian Base Community—a name given to the organization of the Church of the Poor or the Popular Church throughout Latin America

CEDA Nicaragua's Ministry of Education's accelerated primary education program

CELADEC Comision Evangelica Latinoamericana de Educacion Cristiana, Latin American Evangelical Commission on Christian Education—liberal coordinating body of traditional mainstream Protestant Churches for the development of Christian education

CEP Colectivo de Educacion Popular, Popular Education Center—a collective of students and a popular teacher engaged in popular basic education

CEPA Center for Agricultural Development and Advancement—a self-help program founded in 1969 by the Jesuits in Nicaragua to train peasant leaders

Comite de barrio neighborhood committee—a precursor of the *CDC* and *CDS*

CNA La Cruzada Nacional de Alfabetizacion, National Literacy Crusade—Nicaragua's literacy campaign, 1979–80

el comprimiso cristiano The Christian obligation or moral imperative

Conciencia Consciousness and conscience

Concientizacion (Concientizção) Conscientization—to gain *conciencia* of how things are and how they ought to be

Contras Counterrevolutionaries—the name given to the U.S.–backed guerrilla fighters, who resisted the *Sandinista* revolutionary process

coordinadores populares Popular coordinators, the most advanced learners in Nicaragua's literacy campaign who continued to teach their peers

Cursillos Courses, los cursillos de cristiandad, Seminars in Christianity—a retreat movement to motivate Catholics to participate more fully in secular and Church life

Delegado Delegate of the Word—a person trained as a lay leader in the *CEBs*

dirigente Representative of the group

educadores populares Popular teachers, the most advanced students in Nicaragua's literacy campaign who went on to teach in the campaign's follow-up community educational collectives

el encuentro de Solidaridad con El Monsignor Romero The Solidarity meeting with Monsignor Romero, international meetings of *CEB* leaders

ENABAS Empresa Nacional de Alimentos Basicos, National Basic Foods Corporation—the *Sandinista* organization for the purchase and distribution of basic grains

EPB Educacion Popular Basica, Popular Base Education—the Nicaragua popular-education campaign

Expendio Government sponsored food store, established by the *FSLN* after the

Triumph, in poor neighborhoods to provide basic grains for nutrition at the cheapest price

Family of God   Pre-*Vatican II* popular movement in the Catholic Church which encouraged laity participation in parish activities

FMLN   Faribundo Martí Liberacion Nacional, Faribundo Marti National Liberation Front—the revolutionary vanguard and guerrilla fighters engaged in a civil war with the government of El Salvador

FSLN   Frente Sandinista de Liberacion Nacional, National Sandinista Liberation Front, or Frente—*Sandinista* political party, the revolutionary vanguard whose guerrilla members were the principal force in the military overthrow of Anastasio Somoza in Nicaragua

Guatemalidad   Guatemalan national identity

Guardia nacional   National Guard—Anastasio Somoza's military

Guerrilleros   Guerrilla fighters

INSFOP   Instituto para Formacion Permanente, Institute for Permanent Christian Formation—the coordinating office of the regional *CEBs* in Esteli

Jesuits   The Society of Jesus, an order of religious in the Catholic Church, famous as educators throughout the world

JS   Juventud Sandinista, *Sandinista* Youth Organization

JUC   Catholic University Youth, Brazil's union of Catholic university students

ladino   Latino, used here to indicate Hispanic descent rather than Indian

Liberation theology   Theology developed in the Latin American Catholic Church in the last half ot the twentieth century as an expression of solidarity with the poor

La Mano Blanca   The White Hand, an infamous Guatemalan death squad

manzana   A unit corresponding approximately to a neighborhood or *barrio*, contains six blocks

Maryknoll   An order of religious in the Catholic Church, based in the United States and famous for their missionary work in Latin America

MEB   Movimiento Educacao de Base, Base Education Movement—the popular literacy campaign in Brazil, 1961–65

MED   Ministerio de Educacíon, Nicaragua's Ministry of Education

Medellín   Conference of Latin American Catholic bishops held in this city in Columbia in 1968 applied the directives of *Vatican II* to Latin America

MICOIN   Ministerio de Comercio Interior, Nicaraguan Ministry of Internal Commerce

MINDINDRA   Ministerio de Desarrotto Agropecuario e Instituto Nacional de Reforma Agraria, Nicaraguan Ministry of Agricultural Development and Agrarian Reform Institute

MO   Mass Organizations—such as the *CDS*—were fostered by the Sandinistas as enabling the masses to participate in their governance

NBCC   Brazilian National Conference of Catholic Bishops

Padre   Father—the Spanish or Portuguese title given to a Roman Catholic priest

Populorum Progressio   On the Development of Peoples—Pope Paul VI's 1967 social encyclical

presidente   President

el proceso revolucionario   The revolutionary process, revolutionary social transformation

Puebla   Conference of Latin American Catholic bishops to follow *Medellín*, held in this city in Mexico in 1972, furthered the work of *Medellín*

Pueblo   People

responsable   Representative of the group

Sandinista   A member of the *FSLN*, the National Sandinista Liberation Front, the revolutionary vanguard party in Nicaragua

Scholastic theology   Traditional theology of the Catholic Church

Somocismo   Ideology and social institutions supporting, or supported by, the Somoza dictatorship

sostenimiento   Follow-up maintenance to Nicaragua's literacy campaign

Triumph   El Triunfo—the name given to the successful July 19, 1979, revolutionary overthrow of Anastasio Somoza by Nicaraguan supporters of the Revolution

UNAG   Union Nacional de Agricultores y Ganaderos—Sandinista affiliated union of small and medium farmers and ranchers

UNESCO   United Nations Educational, Scientific, and Cultural Organization

United Popular Action Front   Coalition of mass popular political organizations formed in El Salvador in 1974 in opposition to the government

Vatican II   Roman Catholic Church Council, 1962–65, whose purpose was to apply the Church's life and teaching to the modern world

Selected Bibliography

Alas, H. *El Salvador epor que la insurreccion?* San Jose Secretariado permanente de la Comision para la defensa de los derechos humanos en Centroamerica, San Jose, Costa Rica:1982.

Alinsky, S. *Reveille for Radicals.* Chicago: University of Chicago Press, 1946.

———. *Rules for Radicals.* New York: Random House, 1971.

Arnove, R. *Education and Revolution in Nicaragua.* New York: Praeger, 1986.

Arroyo, A., and I. Medina, "Metodologia del analisis coyuntural." *Praxis*, 1, (1982):181–216.

Azevedo, M. C. *Basic Ecclesial Communities in Brazil: The Challenge of a New Way of Being Church.* Trans. J Drury. Washington, DC: Georgetown University Press, 1987.

Bamat, T. "The Catholic Church and Latin American Politics." *Latin American Research Review* 10, No. 3 (1983):219–26.

Barbe, D. *Grace and Power: Base Communities And Nonviolence in Brazil.* Maryknoll, NY: Orbis Books, 1987.

Baum, G. "Symbols and Theology." In *Religion and Alienation.* Toronto: Paulist Press, 1972.

Beckford, J. *Religion in Advanced Industrial Society.* London: Unwin Hyman, 1989.

Bellah, R. "Cultural Values and Corporate Values: Interaction and Interplay." Paper presented at the University of Southern California, Los Angeles, March 8, 1983.

Bellah, R., R. Madsen, W. Sullivan, A. Swidler, and S. Tipton. *Habits of the Heart: Individualism and Commitment in American Life.* Berkeley and Los Angeles: University of California Press, 1985.

Berger, P. *The Sacred Canopy.* Garden City, NY: Doubleday, 1967.

Berger, P., and T. Luckman. *The Social Construction of Reality: A Treatise in the Sociology of Knowledge.* Garden City, NY: Doubleday, 1967.

Bermudez, F. *Death and Resurrection in Guatemala*. Trans. R. Barr. Maryknoll, NY: Orbis Books, 1986.

Berryman, P. "El Salvador: From Evangelization to Insurrection." In *Religion and Political Conflict in Latin America*, ed. D. Levine. Chapel Hill: University of North Carolina Press, 1986.

———. *The Religious Roots of Rebellion: Christians in the Central American Revolutions*. Maryknoll, NY: Orbis Books, 1984.

Biderman, J. "The Development of Capitalism in Nicaragua." *Latin American Perspectives* 10, no. 1 (Winter 1983):7–32.

Black, G. *Garrison Guatemala*. New York: Monthly Review of Books, 1984.

Boff, L. *Jesus Christ Liberator: A Critical Christology for Our Time*. Trans. P. Hughes. Maryknoll, NY: Orbis, 1979.

Bonpane, B. *Guerrillas of Peace: Liberation Theology and the Central American Revolution*. Boston: South End Press, 1985.

———. "The Church and Revolutionary Struggle in Central America." *Latin American Perspectives* 7, no. 2–3 (1980):178–89.

———. "Liberation Theology and the Central American Revolution." Ph.D. diss., University of California, Irvine, 1983.

Booth, J. A. "Celebrating the Demise of Somozismo: Fifty Recent Spanish Sources on the Nicaraguan Revolution." *Latin American Research Review* 17, no. 1 (1982):173–89.

Bowles, S., and H. Gintis. *Schooling in Capitalist America*. New York: Basic Books, 1976.

Bourdieu, P. "Cultural Reproduction and Social Reproduction." In *Knowledge, Education and Cultural Change*, ed. R. Brown. London: Tavistock, 1973.

———. *An Outline of a Theory of Practice*. Cambridge: Cambridge University Press, 1977.

Braverman, H. *Labor and Monopoly Capital: The Degradation of Work in the Twentieth Century*. New York: Monthly Review Press, 1974.

Brown, C. "Literacy in Thirty Hours: Paulo Freire's Literacy Process." *Urban Revolution* 7, no. 3 (1974):245–56.

Bruneau, T. "The Catholic Church and Development in Latin America." *World Development* 8, no. 7–8 (July–August 1980): 535–44.

———. *The Church in Brazil: The Politics of Religion*. Austin: University of Texas Press, 1982.

———. *The Political Transformation of the Brazilian Catholic Church*. New York: Cambridge University Press, 1974

Burke, M. "El sistema de plantación y la proletarización del trabajo agricola en El Salvador." *Estudios Centroamericanos* 31, no. 335–336 (September–October 1976):476–79

Cardenal, E. *El Evangelio en Solentiname*. Managua, Nicaragua: Editorial Nueva Nicaragua, 1983 (1978).

Chicago Religious Task Force on Central America. "Guatemala Presenté." *Basta* (March 1987):43.

Charon, J. *Symbolic Interactionism: An Introduction, An Interpretation, An Integration*. Englewood Cliffs, NJ: Prentice-Hall, 1979.

Chirot, D. *Social Change in the Modern Era*. New York: Harcourt Brace Jovanovich, 1986.

Christenson, J. "Three Themes of Community Development." In *Community Development in America*, ed. J. Christenson and J. Robinson. Ames: Iowa State University Press, 1980.

Cicourel, A. "Notes on the Integrations of Micro- and Macro-Levels of Analysis." In *Advances in Social Theory and Methodology: Toward an Integration of Micro- and Macro-Sociologies*, ed. K. Knorr-Cetina and A. Cicourel. Boston: Routledge and Kegan Paul, 1981.

———. "Some Basic Theoretical Issues in the Assessment of the Child's Performance in Testing and Classroom Settings." In *Language and School Performance*, ed. A. Cicourel et al, 300–351. San Francisco: Academic Press, 1974.

Cleary, G. *Crisis and Change: The Church in Latin America.* Maryknoll, NY: Orbis Books, 1985.

Collins, J. *Nicaragua: What Difference Could a Revolution Make?* New York: Grove Press, 1986.

Collins, R. *Conflict Sociology: Towards an Explanatory Science.* San Francisco: Academic Press, 1975.

Comaroff, J. "White Missionary Christians in South Africa." Colloquium presented at the University of California, Irvine, 1987. Forthcoming.

Comaroff, J., and S. Roberts. *Rules and Processes: The Cultural Logic of Dispute in an African Context.* Chicago: University of Chicago Press, 1981.

Comblin, J. "Os movimentos e a Pastoral Latinoamericano." *Revista Eclesiasta Brasilera* 43(1983): 227–62.

Comision Evangelica Latinoamericana de Educacion Cristiana. *Realidad Latinoamericana y Alternativa Pedagogica.* Lima: La Coordinacion Ecumenica Latinoamericana, 1981.

Coraggio, J. *Nicaragua: Revolucion y Democracia.* Mexico City: Editorial Linea, 1985.

Coraggio, J. and G. Irvin. "Revolution and Democracy in Nicaragua." *Latin American Perspectives*, 12, no. 2. (1985):23–37.

Crump, B. "The Portability of Urban Ties." Paper presented at the Annual Meeting of the American Sociological Association, Chicago, September 1977.

DeJanvry, A. and C. Garranon. "The Dynamics of Rural Poverty in Latin America." *Journal of Peasant Studies*, 4, no. 2 (April 1977):206–16.

Dodson, M. "Liberation Theology and Christian Revolution in Contemporary Latin America." *Journal of Latin American Studies* 11, no. 2 (1979) 203–22.

Dodson, M., and T. S. Montgomery. "The Churches in the Nicaraguan Revolution." In *Nicaragua in Revolution*, ed. T. Walker, 161–80. New York: Praeger, 1982.

Duberman, M. *Black Mountain: An Exploration in Community.* New York: Dutton, 1972.

Durkheim, E. *The Elementary Forms of Religious Life.* New York: Free Press, 1915.

Esquivel, J. *Apuntes sobre Guatemala.* Guatemala: Inedito, 1981.

Evans, P. *Dependent Development.* Princeton: Princeton University Press, 1979.

Fals Borda, O. "Por la Praxis: el problema de como investigar la realidad para transformarla," del Simposio Internacional de Cartegena. *Praxis Centroamericana: Revista Semestral* 1 (1978):209–49.

———. *Science and the Common People.* Dubrovnik, Yugoslavia: International Forum on Participatory Research, 1980.

Felipe and Elena. "The Bible and the Base Communities." *Basta* (June 1987):24–31.

Fields, K. *Revival and Rebellion in Colonial Africa*. Princeton: Princeton University Press, 1985.

Freire, P. "The Adult Education Process as Cultural Action for Freedom." *Harvard Education Review* 40, no. 2 (1970):205–23.

———. "A Dialogue with Apple." Presented at the Dialogue with Freire Conference, University of California, Irvine, July 14, 1987.

———. *Education for a Critical Consciousness*. New York: Seabury, 1973.

———. Interview with author. University of California, Irvine, July 17, 1987.

———. *Pedagogy in Process: Letters to Guinea-Bissau*. Trans. C. St. John Hunter. New York: Seabury Press, 1978.

———. *Pedagogy of the Oppressed*. New York: Continuum, 1970.

———. *The Politics of Education: Culture, Power and Liberation*. South Hadley, MA: Bergin and Garvey, 1985.

Galdamez, P. *Faith of a People: The Life of a Basic Christian Community in El Salvador*. Maryknoll, NY: Orbis Books, 1986.

Gamson, W. *The Strategy of Social Protest*. Homewood, IL: Dorsey Press, 1975.

———. "Understanding the Careers of Challenging Groups." *American Journal of Sociology* 85, no. 5 (1980):1043–60.

Garfinkel, H. *Studies in Ethnomethodology*. Englewood Cliffs. NJ: Prentice-Hall, 1967.

Geertz, C. "Religion as A Cultural System." In *Reader in Comparative Religion: An Anthropological Approach*, ed. W. Less and E. Vogt. New York: Harper and Row, 1972.

Gheerbrand, A. *La iglesia rebelde de America Latina*. Mexico: Ed. Siglo XXI, 1970.

Giddens, A. *Capitalism and Modern Social Theory*. New York: Cambridge University Press, 1971.

Glaser, B. and A. Strauss. *The Discovery of Grounded Theory: Strategies for Qualitative Research*. Chicago: Aldine, 1967.

Goldfrank, W. "Theories of Revolution and Revolution Without Theories: The Case of Mexico." *Theory and Society* 7, no. 1–2 (January–March 1979):135–65.

Goldstone, J. "The Comparative and Historical Study of Revolutions." *Annual Review of Sociology* 8 1982):187–207.

———. "The Weakness of Organization." *American Journal of Sociology* 85, no. 5 (1980):1017–42.

Greenhalgh, K., and M. Gruenke, eds. *The Church Martyred: Guatemala*. Minneapolis: Guatemala Solidarity Committee of Minnesota, 1982.

Gremillion, J., ed. *The Gospel of Peace and Justice: Catholic Social Teaching Since Pope John*. Maryknoll, NY: Orbis Books, 1976.

Gutierrez, G. *A Theology of Liberation: History, Politics and Salvation*. Trans. C. Inda and J. Eagleson. Maryknoll, NY: Orbis, 1973.

Habermas, J. *Knowledge and Human Interests*. Boston: Beacon Press, 1972.

———. "Towards a Reconstruction of Historical Materialism." In *Advances in Social Theory and Methodology: Toward an Integration of Micro- and Macro-Sociologies*, ed. K. Knorr-Cetina and A. Cicourel. Boston: Routledge and Kegan Paul, 1981.

Handy, J. *Gift of the Devil: A History of Guatemala*. Boston: South End Press, 1984.

Harre, R. "Philosophical Aspects of the Macro-Micro Problem." In *Advances in Social Theory and Methodology: Toward an Integration of Micro- and Macro-Sociolo-*

gies, ed. K. Knorr-Cetina and A. Cicourel. Boston: Routledge and Kegan Paul, 1981.

Hewitt, W. E. "Origins and Prospects of the Option for the Poor in Brazilian Communism." *Journal for the Scientific Study of Religion* 28, no. 2 (June 1989):120–35.

Himmelstein, J., and M. Kimmel. "States and Revolutions: The Implications and Limits of Skocpol's Structural Model." *American Journal of Sociology* 86, no. 5, (1981):1145–54.

Hirshon, S. *And Also Teach Them to Read.* Westport, CT: Lawrence Hill and Co., 1983.

Houtart, F. *El cambio social en America Latina.* Bruselas: Oficina Internacional de Investigaciones Sociales de FERES, 1964.

Hungs, F. J. *Comunidad y Catequesis: Teoria y praxis para la formacion de Catequistas.* Trans. Ramiro Reiz. Santander, Spain: Editorial Sal Tarrae, 1982.

Hynds, P. "La Lucha Ideologica Dentro de la Iglesia Catolica Nicaraguense." In *Religión y Revolución en Nicaragua.* Managua: Nueva Nicaragua, 1980.

Ileto, R. *Pasyon and Revolution: Popular Movements in the Philippines, 1840–1910.* Manila: Ateneo de Manila University Press, 1979.

Janowitz, M. *The Community Press in an Urban Setting.* Chicago: University of Chicago Press, 1952.

Jara Holiday, O. *Educacion Popular: La dimension educativa de la accion politica.* Panama: Centro de Estudios y Accion Social de Panama, 1981.

———. "Teoria y Practica: Conciencia de clases, metodo dialectico y educacion popular," *Praxis*, 2 (1983):295–330.

Kadushin, C. "The Friends and Supporters of Psychotherapy: On Social Circles in Urban Life." *American Sociological Review* 31, no. 6 (December 1966):786–802.

Kincaid, D. "Peasants into Rebels: Community and Class in Rural El Salvador." *Comparative Studies in Society and History* 29 (July 1987):466–94.

Knorr-Cetina, K. "Introduction: the Micro-Sociological Challenge of Macro-Sociology"; "Towards a Reconstruction of Social Theory and Methodology." In *Advances in Social Theory and Methodology: Toward an Integration of Micro- and Macro-Sociologies*, ed. K. Knorr-Cetina and A. Cicourel. Boston: Routledge and Kegan Paul, 1981.

Knorr-Cetina, K. and A. Cicourel. eds. *Advances in Social Theory and Methodology: Toward an Integration of Micro- and Macro-Sociologies.* Boston: Routledge and Kegan Paul, 1981.

Kuhn, T. *The Structure of Scientific Revolutions.* Chicago: The University of Chicago Press, 1962.

Lan, D. *Guns and Rain: Guerrillas and Spirit Mediums in Zimbabwe.* Berkeley and Los Angeles: University of California Press, 1985.

Lanternari, V. *The Religions of the Oppressed: A Study of Modern Messianic Cults.* Trans. L. Sergio. New York: New American Library, 1965.

Latorre Cabal, H. *La revolucion de la Iglesia Latino Americana.* Mexico City: Editorial Joaquin Mortiz, 1969.

Laue, J. and G. Cormick. "The Ethics of Intervention in Community Disputes." In *The Ethics of Social Intervention*, ed. G. Bermant, H. Kehman, and D. Warwick. New York: John Wiley and Sons, 1978.

Leaf, M. J. *Man, Mind and Science: A History of Anthropology*. New York: Columbia University Press, 1979.

Le Boterf, G. "Investigacion-Accion y Educacion Popular en una Sociedad en Transicion." Seminar presented on the formation of base promoters in literacy programmes in the Principal Education Project in Latin America and the Caribbean, Managua, Nicaragua, December 10–16, 1981.

Lernoux, P. *Cry of the People*. Garden City, NY: Doubleday 1980.

———. "The Pope and Latin America." *Catholic Agitator* 19, no. 5 (June 1989):3–6.

Levine, D. "Basic Christian Communities in Latin America: Their Nature and Significance." In *Churches and Politics in Latin America*, ed D. Levine. Beverly Hills, CA: Sage, 1989.

———., ed. *Religion and Political Conflict in Latin America*. Chapel Hill: University of North Carolina Press, 1986.

Lifton, J. *Thought Reform and the Psychology of Totalism*. A Study of Brainwashing in China. New York: Norton, 1961.

Lipset, S., M. Trow, and J. Coleman. *Union Democracy: The Internal Politics of the International Typographical Union*. New York: Free Press, 1956.

Madriz, C. "Popular Culture, Base Communities and Pentecostals Churches in Brazil." Paper presented at the Annual Meeting of the Society for the Scientific Study of Religion, Chicago, October 28–30, 1988.

Mainwaring, S. *The Catholic Church and Politics in Brazil, 1916–1985*. Stanford: Stanford University Press, 1986.

———. "Grassroots Catholic Groups and Politics in Brazil." Paper presented at the Annual Meeting of the Society for the Scientific Study of Religion, Chicago, October 28–30, 1988.

———. "Grass-roots Catholic Groups and Politics in Brazil." In *The Progressive Church in Latin America*, ed. S. Mainwaring and A. Wilde. South Bend, IN: University of Notre Dame Press, 1989.

Mainwaring, S., and A. Wilde, eds. *The Progressive Church in Latin America*. South Bend, IN: University of Notre Dame Press, 1989.

Mannheim, K. *Freedom, Power, and Democratic Planning*. London: Routledge and Kegan Paul, 1950.

———. *Ideology and Utopia*. New York: Harcourt, Brace and World, 1936.

Marin, A. R. *Esquemas de los Cursillos de Cristiandad*. Madrid: Euroamerica S.A., 1963.

Marins, J. *Comunidade eclesial de base: curso fundamental*. Buenos Aires: Editorial Bonum, 1972.

———. "Comunidades eclesias de base no America Latina." *Concilium* 104 (1975).

———. *Entrenamiento Intensivo sobre Comunidades de Base*. Buenos Aires: Editorial Bonum, 1971.

———. *Iglesia y conflictividad social en America Latina: reflexion pastoral a partir de la CEB*. Bogota: Ediciones Paulina, 1975.

———. *Modelos de Iglesia: CEB en America Latina, hacia un modelo liberador*. Bogota: Ediciones Paulina, 1976.

Marx, K. "The Eighteenth Brumaire of Napoleon Bonaparte." In *The Marx-Engels Reader*, ed. R. Tucker. New York: Norton, 1972.

McCarthy, J. and M. Zald. "Resource Mobilization and Social Movements: A Partial Theory." *American Journal of Sociology* 82, no. 6 (1976):1212–42.

Mead, G. H. *Mind, Self and Society*. Chicago: University of Chicago Press, 1962.

Melendez, G., and P. Richard. *La iglesia de los pobres en America Central*. San Jose, Costa Rica: DEI, 1982.

Metzger, D., and K. Ortiz. "Getting Understanding Through Border Work." University of California, Irvine and Rosebridge Graduate School of Integrative Psychology, 1985. Paper.

Metzger, D. & G. Williams. "Tenejapa Medicine I: The Curer." In *Reader in Comparative Religion: An Anthropological Approach*, ed. W. Lessa and E. Vogt. New York: Harper and Row, 1972.

Michels, R. *Political Parties: A Sociological Study of the Oligarchical Tendencies of Modern Democracy*. Glencoe, IL: Free Press, 1949. Reprint. New York: Free Press, 1962.

Miller, V. *Between Struggle and Hope: The Nicaraguan Literacy Crusade*. Boulder, CO: Westview Press, 1985.

———. "The Nicaraguan Literacy Crusade." In *Nicaragua in Revolution*, ed. T. Walker. New York: Praeger, 1982.

Ministry of Education. *El Amanecer del Pueblo*. Managua: Ministry of Education, 1980.

Montgomery, T. "Cross and Rifle: Revolution and the Church in El Salvador and Nicaragua." *Journal of International Affairs* 36, no. 2 (1982–83):209–21.

Monteith, M. K. "Paulo Freire's Literacy Method." *Journal of Reading* 20, no. 7 (1977):628–31.

Mulligan, J. "The Historical Significance of Nicaragua." *Monthly Review* 39, no. 8 (January 1988):1–10.

Neuhouser, K. "The Radicalization of the Brazilian Catholic Church in Comparative Perspective." *American Sociological Review* 54, no. 2 (April 1989):233–44.

Neumann, E. *The Origins and History of Consciousness*. Trans. R. Hall. Princeton: Princeton University Press, 1970.

Oberschall, A. *Social Conflicts and Social Movements*. Englewood Cliffs, NJ: Prentice-Hall, 1973.

Ocampo, C. *Y Tambien ensenenles a leer*. Managua: Nueva Nicaragua, 1984.

O'Dea, T. "Religion in Conflict." Chap. 5 in *The Sociology of Religion*, Englewood Cliffs, NJ: Prentice-Hall, 1966.

Ortiz, K. *Accounts of Desperate Times: Six Cuban Refugee Life Histories*. Ann Arbor, MI: University Microfilms, 1984.

Paige, J. *Agrarian Revolution: Social Movement and Export Agriculture in the Underdeveloped World*. New York: Free Press, 1975.

———."Cotton & Revolution in Nicaragua." In *States versus Markets in the World System*, ed. P. Evans, D. Rueschemyer, and E. Stephens. Beverly Hills: Sage Publications, 1985.

Parenti, M. *The Sword and the Dollar*. New York: St. Martin's Press, 1989.

Pinard, M. *The Rise of a Third Party: A Study in Crisis Politics*. Englewood Cliffs, NJ: Prentice-Hall, 1971.

Planas, R. *Liberation Theology: The Political Expression of Religion*. Kansas City, MO: Sheed and Ward, 1989.

Pope Paul VI. "Populorum Progressio: On the Development of Peoples" (March 26, 1967). In *The Gospel of Peace and Justice: Catholic Social Teaching Since Pope John*, ed. J. Gremellion. Maryknoll, NY: Orbis Books, 1976.

Prendes, J. "Revolutionary Struggle and Church Commitment: The Case of El Salvador." *Social Compass* 30, no. 2–3 (1983):261–98.

Randall, M. *Cristianos en la revolucion*. Managua: Nueva Nicaragua, 1983.

———. *Cristianos en la revolucion* manuscript. Library of El Centro Antonio Valdivieso, Managua, Nicaragua.

Radford Ruether, R. "Ecumenism in Central America." *Christianity and Crisis* 49, no. 10, (August, 1989):208–12.

Ranger, T. *Peasant Consciousness and Guerrilla War in Zimbabwe: A Comparative Study*. Berkeley and Los Angeles: University of California Press, 1985.

Ribeiro de Oliveira, P. "Conflict and Change in the Latin American Church." Plenary Session presented at the Annual Meeting of the Society for the Scientific Study of Religion, Chicago, October 28–30, 1988.

Rivera y Damas, A. Speech given at a special session of the Latin American Studies Association 15th International Congress, Miami, December 4–6, 1989.

Robinson, J. "The Conflict Approach." In *Community Development in America*, ed. J. Christenson and J. Robinson. Ames: Iowa State University Press, 1980.

Rodriguez, D. "La situacion de un sacerdote que trabajar directamente en comunidades cristianas de base, afronta la tension entre el laico y la jerarquia," in Reports on the ecclesial meeting held August 28, to September 2, 1976, "El laico en el compromiso social: VI encuentro regional de justicia y pas, Mexico, Centroamerica y Panama." Transcribed by the Regional Secretary of Justice and Peace of the University of Central America in El Salvador. Manuscript in library of the Centro Antonio Valdevieso, Managua, Nicaragua.

Romanucci-Ross, L. *Mead's Other Manus: Phenomenology of the Encounter*. South Hadley, MA: Bergin and Garvey, 1985.

Rothschild, J. and A. Whitt. *The Cooperative Workplace: Potentials and Dilemmas of Organizational Democracy and Participation*. New York: Cambridge University Press, 1986.

Roxborough, I. *Theories of Underdevelopment*. London: Macmillan, 1979.

Sahlins, M. *Culture and Practical Reason*. Chicago: University of Chicago Press, 1976.

Salert, B. *Revolutions and Revolutionaries*. New York: Elsevier, 1976.

Sargeant, W. *Battle for the Mind*. Garden City, NY: Doubleday, 1957.

Secretariado Diocesano Ciudad Real. *Cursillos de Cristiandad: Realidades y Experiencias*. Madrid: Euroamaerica S.A., 1961.

Segundo, J. L. *The Community Called Church*. Maryknoll, NY: Orbis, 1973.

Serra, L. "The Sandinista Mass Organizations," in *Nicaragua in Revolution*, ed. T. Walker, 95–114. New York: Praeger, 1982.

Sierra Pop, O. "The Church and Social Conflicts in Guatemala." *Social Compass* 30, no. 2–3 (1983) 317–48.

Skocpol, T. *States and Social Revolution*. New York: Cambridge University Press, 1979.

———. "Wallerstein's World Capitalist System: A Theoretical and Historical Critique." *American Journal of Sociology* 82, no. 5, (1977) 1075–90.

Skocpol, T., and M. Somers. "Uses of Comparative History in Macrosocial Analysis." *Comparative Studies in Society and History* 22 no. 2 (April 1980):174–97.

Smith, Carol. *Regional Analysis.* New York: Academic Press, 1976.

Smutko, G. *Pastoral Indigenista: Experiencia entre los Miskitos.* Bogota: Ediciones Paulina, 1975.

Somers, M. and W. Goldfrank. "The Limits of Agronomic Determinism: A Critique of Paige's Agrarian Revolutions." *Comparative Studies in Society and History* 21, no. 3 (July 1979):443–58.

Stinchcombe, A. *Theoretical Methods in Social History: Studies in Social Discontinuity.* San Francisco: Academic Press, 1978.

Swanson, G. *Religion and Regimes: A Sociological Account of the Reformation.* Ann Arbor: University of Michigan Press, 1967.

Taylor, J. *From Modernization to Modes of Production: A Critique of the Sociologies of Development and Underdevelopment.* London: Macmillan, 1983.

Tillich, P. *Dynamics of Faith.* New York: Harper and Row, 1957.

Tilly, C. *From Mobilization to Revolution.* Reading, MA: Addison-Wesley, 1978.

——. The Rebellious Century. Cambridge: Harvard University Press, 1975.

Torres, R. M. *De Alfabetizando a Maestro Popular: La Post-Alfabetizacion en Nicaragua.* Managua: Instituto nacional de investigaciones economicas y sociales, 1983.

——. "La Post-Alfabetizacion como proceso social: el casa de Nicaragua." Paper presented at the Fifth Central American Sociology Congress, "La Sociologia antes la crisis centroamericana," San Jose, Costa Rica, November 22, 1982.

Trimberger, E. "A Theory of Elite Revolutions." In *Revolutions: Theoretical, Comparative and Historical Studies,* ed. J. Goldstone. San Diego: Harcourt Brace Jovanovich, 1986.

Truemann, B. "Cultural Insurrection in Nicaragua." Boston, 1981. Mimeograph.

——. "Nicaragua's Second Revolution." *Christianity and Crisis* 41, no. 17 (1981):291–98.

Tunnermann Bernheim, C. *Hacia Una Nueva Educacion en Nicaragua.* Managua: Ediciones Distribudora Cultura S. A., 1983.

Turner, J. "Toward a Sociological Theory of Motivation." *American Sociological Review,* 52, no. 1 (February 1987):15–27.

Tyson, B. "Brazil: End of an Era?" *Christianity and Crisis* 49, no. 9 (1989):193–94.

Van Vugt, J. "Christian Base Communities." *Ecumenist* 24, no. 1 (1985):1–8.

Vega, Bishop Juan Ramos, Assesor. "Movimiento y agrupaciones de laicos en Nicaragua y su insercion en la pastoral." "Work realized at the call of the Episcopal Conference of Nicaragua for the Bishops/Laity Dialogue of August 17–19, 1977, in Matagalpa, Nicaragua," including "Anexo: Respuestas a la encuesta hecha entre los distintos movimientos y agrupaciones de laicos." Manuscript in the archives of the library of El Centro Antonio Valdivieso, Managua, Nicaragua.

Vieira, P. A. *Conciencia e Realidade Nacional.* Rio de Janeiro: Ministerio da Educacao e Cultura; Instituto Superior de Estudos Brasileiros, 1960.

Vilas, C. "Producion de lo nuevo y la reproducion de lo viejo: Educacion, ideologia, y poder popular en Nicaragua." Paper presented at the Fifth Congress of Central American Sociology, San Jose, Costa Rica, November 1982.

Wallerstein, I. *The Capitalist World Economy.* New York: Cambridge University Press, 1979.

Walker, G. "Social Networks and Territory in a Commuter Village, Bond Head, Ontario." *Canadian Geographer* 21 (Winter 1977):329–50.

Walker, T. ed. *Nicaragua in Revolution*. New York: Praeger, 1982.

Walton, J. *Reluctant Rebels: Comparative Studies of Revolution and Underdevelopment*. New York: Columbia University Press, 1984.

Wanderly, J. *Educar para transformar: Educacao popular, Igreja Catolica e politica no movimento de educacao de base*. Petropolis, Brazil: Editor Vozes, 1984.

Warren, R. *The Community in America*. Chicago: Rand McNally, 1963.

Weber, M. *Economy and Society*. Ed. G. Roth and C. Wittich. New York: Bedminster Press, 1968.

———. *From Max Weber: Essays in Sociology*. Trans. and ed. H. Gerth and C. Wright Mills. New York: Oxford University Press, 1946.

———. *The Protestant Ethic and the Spirit of Capitalism*. London: Allen and Unwin, 1904.

Wellman, B., and B. Leighton. "Networks, Neighborhoods, and Communities: Approaches to the Study of the Community Question." In *New Perspectives on the American Community*, edited R. Warren and L. Lyons. Chicago: Dorsey Press, 1988.

Wheaton, P. "The Third Assembly of Salvadoran Ecclesial Base Communities." *Basta* (March 1987):35–40.

White, H. "Agency as Control." In *Principals and Agents: The Structure of Business*, ed. J. Pratt and R. Zeckhaufer. Boston: Graduate School of Business Administration, 1985.

Willis, P. "Cultural Production is Different from Cultural Reproduction is Different from Social Reproduction is Different from Reproduction." *Interchange* 12, no. 2 (1981):48–63.

———. *Learning to Labor: How Working Class Kids Get Working Class Jobs*. New York: Columbia University Press, 1977.

Winn, D. *The Manipulated Mind*. London: Octagon Press, 1983.

Winson, A. "Class Structures and Agrarian Transition in Central America." *Latin American Perspectives* 5, no. 4 (Fall 1978):27–48.

Wolf, E. "Peasant Rebellion and Revolution." In *Revolutions*, ed. J. Goldstone. San Diego: Harcourt Brace Jovanovich, 1986.

———. *Peasant Wars of the Twentieth Century*. New York: Harper and Row, 1969.

Zald, M. "Issues in the Theory of Social Movements." *Current Perspectives in Social Movements*, 1 (1980):61–72.

Index

About the Author

JOHANNES P. VAN VUGT is versed and credentialed in a wide range of disciplines, including history, education, religious studies, anthropology, sociology, and psychology. He is currently Assistant Professor in the Department of Sociology and Anthropology at Fordham University in New York City, where he continues his research on community-based organizations.